When Rain Clouds Gather

and Related Readings

McDougal Littell
A HOUGHTON MIFFLIN COMPANY

Evanston, Illinois Boston Dallas

Acknowledgments

John Johnson Limited: *When Rain Clouds Gather* by Bessie Head. Copyright © 1968 by Bessie Head. Reprinted by permission of John Johnson Limited for the Estate of Bessie Head.

East African Educational Publishers Ltd.: "The Rain Came," from *Land Without Thunder* by Grace Ogot. Copyright © 1968 by Grace Ogot. Reprinted by permission of East African Educational Publishers Ltd.

South Dakota Review: "I Am Crying from Thirst" by Alonzo Lopez, first appeared in *South Dakota Review*, Summer 1969. Reprinted by permission of South Dakota Review.

Algonquin Books of Chapel Hill: Excerpt from *Waiting for Rain: A Farmer's Story* by Dan Butterworth. Copyright © 1992 by Dan Butterworth. Reprinted by permission of Algonquin Books of Chapel Hill, a division of Workman Publishing.

Faber and Faber Limited: "Crackling Day," from *Tell Freedom* by Peter Abrahams. Copyright 1954 by Peter Abrahams. Reprinted by permission of the publisher, Faber and Faber Limited.

Viking Penguin: "Some Monday for Sure," from *Selected Stories* by Nadine Gordimer. Copyright © 1965 by Nadine Gordimer. Used by permission of Viking Penguin, a division of Penguin Books USA Inc.

Continued on page 288.

Cover illustration by Michael Steirnagle.
Author photo: T. Goldblatt/Camera Press/Globe Photos.

ISBN 0-395-77546-9

456789—QNT—03 02 01 00

Contents

When Rain Clouds Gather

Bessie Head

NOTE

Bantu languages use prefixes thus:
Botswana is the name of the country;
The Batswana are the Tswana people who
live there;
A Motswana is an individual member of the
Tswana tribe.

Chapter 1

The little Barolong village swept right up to the border fence. One of the huts was built so close that a part of its circular wall touched the barbed-wire fencing. In this hut a man had been sitting since the early hours of dawn. He was waiting until dark when he would try to sprint across the half-mile gap of no-man's-land to the Botswana border fence and then on to whatever illusion of freedom lay ahead. It was June and winter and bitterly cold, and his legs were too long to allow for pacing in the cramped space of the hut. Every half hour the patrol van of the South African border police sped past with sirens wailing, and this caused an unpleasant sensation in his stomach.

I'll soon have a stomach-ache if I go on like this, he thought.

His nerves weren't so good, too easily jangled by the irritations of living. In fact, the inner part of him was a jumble of chaotic discord, very much belied by his outer air of calm, lonely self-containment. The only way you could sense this inner discord was through a trick he had of slightly averting his face as though no man was his brother or worthy of trust. Otherwise, his face was rather pleasing to the eye. It was often wryly amused. Its general expression was one of absorbed, attentive listening. His long thin falling-away cheekbones marked him as a member of either the Xhosa or Zulu tribe.

Towards noon, when there was a lull in the wailing sirens, the old man who owned the hut pushed open the door, letting in a shaft of sunlight. He held in his hands a steaming bowl of thick porridge. The man by now had a dreadful stomach-ache, and the sight of the food did not immediately please him.

"Well, how are you, son?" the old man asked.

"I'm all right," the man lied. It did not seem quite dignified to admit that he had stomach trouble.

"I've brought you a little food," the old man said.

"Thank you," the man said. "But could I go out for a while and stretch my legs?" He had to ease the painful knots in his stomach.

"It's not safe," the old man said. "I can't guarantee who may or may not be a spy. Once you are caught here it will make it unsafe for those who come on behind. I would no doubt go to jail too."

The young man was bent over the small hand-carved stool on which he sat, and the old man thought he might be cold.

"Why not take a little brandy?" he asked sympathetically. "I know a place nearby, and I can send for some if you want it."

The man looked up, relieved, and nodded his head. He took out a pound note and handed it to the old man. The old man smiled widely. He had not known of one fugitive yet who did not need it. Besides, with a little brandy inside they soon became talkative, and he liked all the stories. He stored them up against the day when he would be free to surprise his village with his vast fund of information on fugitives. He closed the door and shuffled away. A dog barked nearby. There was the chatter of women's voices, and music and singing. A child began to cry loudly. Men laughed, and the man in the hut was briefly surprised that a whole village could live in the wail of those sirens that had tied his stomach in such tight knots. Soon the old man shuffled back again. Because relief was near at hand he noticed how the dust of the mud floor rose up and shimmered and danced in the sunlight as the old man pushed open the door. The old man had not only the brandy but a bowl of food for himself as well. It pleased the young man in the shadows that he did not close the door because as soon as he had taken a few careful sips from the bottle, he could clearly discern the gentle, interweaving dance pattern of the sunlit dust. The slow, almost breathless rhythm eased away the knots of stomach trouble, and he unconsciously smiled to himself in this sudden warm glow of expansive relief that was now his abdomen.

Noting this the old man said, "I say, son, what's your name?"

"Makhaya," the young man replied.

The old man screwed up his eyes, perplexed. The sound and meaning of the name were unfamiliar to him. Tswana-speaking tribes dominated the northern Transvaal.

"I don't know it," the old man said, shaking his head.

"It's Zulu," the young man said. "I'm a Zulu." And he laughed sarcastically at the thought of calling himself a Zulu.

"But you speak Tswana fluently," the old man persisted.

Quite drunk by now the young man said rather crazily, "Yes, we Zulus are like that. Since the days of Shaka we've assumed that the whole world belongs to us; that's why we trouble to learn any man's language. But look here, old man, I'm no tribalist. My parents are—that's why they saddled me with this foolish name. Why not call me Samuel or Johnson, because I'm no tribalist."

"Jo!" said the old man, using a Tswana expression of surprise. "And what's wrong with the tribe?"

"I have a list of grievances against it. I haven't got time to go into them now . . ." He paused, trying to collect his thoughts in the haze of brandy that was clouding his brain. "Makhaya," he said. "That tribal name is the wrong one for me. It is for one who stays home, yet they gave it to me and I have not known a day's peace and contentment in my life."

"It's because of education," the old man said, nodding his head wisely. "They should not have given you the education. Take away the little bit of education and you will be only too happy to say, 'Mama, please find me a tribal girl and let us plough.' It's only the education that turns a man away from his tribe."

The conversation threatened to become a vast, meaningless, rambling digression. Good storyteller that he was, the old man brought it back to the main points at hand. Why was the young man here? What was he fleeing from? A jail sentence, perhaps?

The young man looked at him suspiciously. "I'm just out of jail," he said. He closed the brandy bottle and picked up the bowl of porridge. And then some anxiety seemed to jolt him for he put the bowl down again, searched the inside pocket of his coat, and took out a little scrap of paper. He struck a match and burned the paper. Then he picked up the bowl of porridge and would not utter another word. The old man was left to put two and two together. Perhaps scraps of paper and jail sentences were the same thing in the young man's mind. Why did he jump so at the thought of one tiny scrap? And what was this about tribalism? What about the white man who was the only recognized enemy of everyone?

"Oh, so you have no complaints about the white man?" the old man said, struggling to pry some information out of the tightly shut mouth.

The young man only turned his face slightly, yet the light of laughter danced in his eyes.

"Ha, I see now," the old man said, pretending disappointment. "You are running away from tribalism. But just ahead of you is the worst tribal country in the world. We Barolongs are neighbours of the Batswana, but we cannot get along with them. They are a thick-headed lot who think no further than this door. Tribalism is meat and drink to them."

The young man burst out laughing. "Oh, Papa," he said. "I just want to step on free ground. I don't care about people. I don't care about anything, not even the white man. I want to feel what it is like to live in a free country and then maybe some of the evils in my life will correct themselves."

The wail of the approaching sirens sounded again. After they had swept past, the old man left the hut, closing the door behind him. Makhaya was left alone with his thoughts, and since these threatened to trouble him, he kept on numbing them with a little brandy sipped straight from the bottle.

The sun set early in winter and by seven o'clock it was pitch dark. Makhaya made ready to cross the patch of no-man's-land. The two border fences were seven-foot-high barriers of close, tautly drawn barbed wire. He waited in the hut until he heard the patrol van pass. Then he removed his heavy overcoat and stuffed it into a large leather bag. He stepped out of the hut and pitched the leather bag over the fence, grasped hold of the barbed wire, and heaved himself up and over. Picking up his bag, he ran as fast as he could across the patch of ground to the other fence, where he repeated the performance. Then he was in Botswana.

In his anxiety to get as far away from the border as fast as possible, he hardly felt the intense, penetrating cold of the frosty night. For almost half an hour he sped, blind and deaf and numbed to anything but his major fear. The wail of the siren brought him to an abrupt halt. It sounded shockingly near and he feared that his crashing pace would draw attention to himself. But the lights of the patrol van swept past and he knew, from timing the patrols throughout the long torturous day, that he had another half hour of safety ahead of him. As he relaxed a little, his mind grasped the fact that he had been sucking in huge gulps of frozen air and that his lungs were flaming with pain. He removed the heavy coat from the bag and put it on. He also took a few careful sips from the brandy bottle and then continued on his way at a more leisurely pace.

He had not walked more than a few paces when he again came to an abrupt halt. The air was full of the sound of bells, thousands and thousands of bells, tinkling and tinkling with a purposeful, monotonous rhythm. Yet there was not a living thing in sight to explain where the sound was coming from. He was quite sure that around him and in front of him were trees and more trees, thorn trees that each time he approached too near ripped at his clothes. But how to explain the bells, unearthly sounding bells in an apparently unlived-in wasteland?

Oh, God, I'm going crazy, he thought.

He looked up at the stars. They winked back at him, silently, blandly. He could even make out some of the star patterns of the southern constellations. Surely, if his mind was suddenly disordered through the tensions of the day, the stars would appear disordered too? Surely everything became mixed up to a person who had just lost his mind? He shook his head, but the bells continued their monotonous, rhythmic tinkling. He knew some pretty horrifying stories about tribal societies and their witch doctors who performed their ghoulish rites by night. But witch doctors were human, and nothing, however odd and perverse, need be feared if it was human. Taking this as a possible explanation of the bells restored his balance, and he continued on his way, keeping an alert eye open for the fires or huts of the witch doctors.

Soon he saw a fire in the bush, a small bit of self-contained light in the overwhelming darkness. He headed straight for it, and as he approached, the flickering, crackling light outlined the shape of two mud huts and the forms of a woman and a child. It was the woman who looked up as she became aware of approaching footsteps. He stood still, not wishing to alarm her. She appeared to be very old. Her small eyes were completely sunk in the wrinkles of her face. The child was a girl of about ten who kept her head bent, idly drawing a pattern with a stick on the ground. He greeted the old woman in Tswana, politely calling her mother in a quiet, reassuring voice.

She did not return the greeting. Instead she demanded, "Yes, what do you want?" She had a loud, shrill, uncontrolled voice, and he disliked her immediately.

"I was looking for shelter for the night," he said.

She kept quiet, yet stared fixedly at the direction from which his voice came. Then she burst out in that loud, jarring voice, "I say you are one of the spies from over the border."

Since he did not respond she became quite excited, raising her voice even louder. "Why else do people wander about at night, unless they are spies? All the spies in the world are coming into our country. I tell you, you are a spy! You are a spy!"

It was the shouting that unnerved him. The border was still very near, and at any moment now the patrol van would pass.

"How can you embarrass me like this?" he said in a quiet, desperate voice. "Are women of your country taught to shout at men?"

"I'm not shouting," she shrilled, but in a slightly lower voice. His words and consistently quiet speech were beginning to impress her.

"Well, my ears must be deceiving me, mother," he

said, amused. "Tell me whether you can offer me shelter or not. I'm no spy. I've just lost my way in the darkness."

The fixed stare never wavered. She said, curtly, "I have a spare hut. You may use it but only for tonight. You must also pay. I want ten shillings."

She held out a shrivelled old hand, cold and hard with years and years of labour. He stepped towards the fire and handed her a ten-shilling note. She reached behind her for a small carved stool and said, "Sit here. The child will sweep the hut and put down some blankets."

The child stood up obediently and disappeared into one of the huts. He sat down opposite the crude, rude phenomenon who continued staring at him. The wail of the patrol siren again sounded quite near, almost behind his back. He held her glance calmly.

"I know you are a spy," she said. "You are running away from them."

He smiled. "Perhaps you just want to annoy me. But as you can see, I'm not easily annoyed."

"Where do you come from?" she asked.

"From over the border," he said. "I have an appointment to start work in this country tomorrow."

"Why didn't you come by train?" she asked suspiciously.

"But my home is so near, in the Barolong village," he lied.

She turned her head and spat on the ground as an eloquent summing up of what she thought of him. Then she sat with her head averted as though she had abruptly dismissed him from her thoughts. The bells were still tinkling away.

"What are all those bells for?" he asked.

"They are tied around the necks of the cattle because they are grazing freely in the bush," she said.

He felt ashamed at the thought of how they had

terrified him and they were only cow bells. He also wanted to laugh out loud, and to suppress this he said conversationally, "I'm not an owner of cattle. I suppose the bells are there to locate them if they get lost?"

"Of course," she said scornfully. "Cattle wander a great distance while grazing."

Meanwhile the child had crept quietly back to the fireside. Half-consciously his gaze wandered in her direction, and he was startled to find the child looking at him with a full bold stare. There was something very unchildlike about it and it displeased him. His glance flickered back to the old woman. She was staring again and he even imagined that he saw a gleam in the sunken old eyes.

My God, he thought, what a pair of vultures they are.

Aloud he said, "Is the room ready now, mother?"

She merely turned and pointed to one of the huts. He stood up immediately, relieved to be rid of their unpleasant company. He struck a match as he entered the dark hut. It seemed to be a storage shed. A large grain basket stood in one corner, and there were a number of earthenware pots encircling the room. A space had been cleared on the floor on which were placed wide square covers made of animal skins. He struck another match to take a better look at what he was to sleep on. The feel of it was like thick soft velvet, squares upon squares of the sewn-together skins of hundreds of wild animals. He only removed his shoes and overcoat. The overcoat he flung over the top cover for extra warmth. The bed seemed well worth ten shillings to him because it was very warm.

He lay on his back staring up at the dark, too tense to sleep. A good gulp of brandy would have knocked him out cold but he dared not touch it. He distrusted the suspicious old hag. She seemed to know too much about the border. What would prevent her from stepping down there and informing the police? There was good money in it, if she knew about that too. A cold sweat broke out on him as he imagined her at the fence, shouting at the patrol van. And what about the child and her awful, unchildlike stare? He listened alertly to their every movement. For a time there was a low murmured conversation, and then he heard the fire being scraped out. Then the door of the next hut was pushed open. The old hag coughed a bit. There was more murmured conversation and a brief silence. Then the door was opened again and he could tell that it was the child who had gone out because the old hag was coughing inside.

He lay quite still as the door of his hut was carefully and quietly pushed open by the child and equally quietly and carefully closed behind her. She dropped lightly down on her knees and moved her hands over the covers until they reached his face.

"What do you want?" he asked.

The hands darted back and there was a brief silence; then she said, "You know."

"I don't," he said.

She kept quiet as though puzzling this out. At last she said, "My grandmother won't mind as long as you pay me."

"Go away," he said, abashed, humiliated. "You're just a child."

But she just sat there and would not move. He really could not stand it. He raised himself and struck a match and took out a ten-shilling note and handed it to her.

"Here's the money," he said fiercely. "Now go away."

Her eyes were wide and uncomprehending in the brief glare of the match, but she grasped the note and fled. From the hut next door he heard the brief plaintive explanation of the child and the loud surprised chatter of the old woman.

"You mean he gave you the money for nothing?" she said, beside herself with excitement. "This is a miracle! I have not yet known a man who did not regard a woman as a gift from God! He must be mad! I knew it all along in my heart that he was mad! Let us lock the door to protect ourselves from the madman!"

What a loathsome woman, he thought, and yet how naïve she was in her evil. He had known many such evils in his lifetime. He thought they were created by poverty and oppression, and he had spent the last two years in jail in the belief that, in some way, a protest would help to set the world right. It was the mentality of the old hag that ruined a whole continent—some sort of clinging, ancestral, tribal belief that a man was nothing more than a grovelling sex organ, that there was no such thing as privacy of soul and body, and that no ordinary man would hesitate to jump on a mere child.

He had sisters at home, one almost the same age as the child and some a few years older. But he was the eldest in the family, and according to custom he had to be addressed as "Buti", which means "Elder Brother", and treated with exaggerated respect. As soon as his father died he made many changes in the home, foremost of which was that his sisters should address him by his first name and associate with him as equals and friends. When his mother had protested he had merely said, "Why should men be brought up with a false sense of superiority over women? People can respect me if they wish, but only if I earn it."

For all his strange new ideas, the family had not wanted to part with him. In fact he had left his mother in a state of complete collapse, and though at the time he had pretended to be unmoved by all the tears and sighs, it was all this that had made him drink brandy throughout the afternoon. His reasons for leaving were simple: he could not marry and have children in a country where black men were called "boy" and "dog" and "kaffir". The continent of Africa was vast without end and he simply felt like moving out of a part of it that was mentally and spiritually dead through the constant perpetuation of false beliefs.

I might like it here, was his last thought before falling into a deep, exhausted sleep.

It was not yet dawn when he arose and left. In the faint early light he saw a little footpath leading away from the huts, and because it wound its way northward and away from the border, he decided to follow it in the hope that it would lead him somewhere.

At first not a thing stirred around him. It was just his own self, his footsteps and the winding footpath. Even the sunrise took him by surprise. Somehow he had always imagined the sun above hills, shining down into valleys and waking them up. But here the land was quite flat, and the sunshine crept along the ground in long shafts of gold light. It kept on pushing back the darkness that clung around the trees, and always the huge splash of gold was split into shafts by the trees. Suddenly, the sun sprang clear of all entanglements, a single white pulsating ball, dashing out with one blow the last traces of the night. So sudden and abrupt was the sunrise that the birds had to pretend they had been awake all the time. They set up a shrill piercing clamour all at once, thousands and thousands of them. For all their clamour they turned out to be small dun-coloured creatures with speckled dun-coloured breasts, and their flight into the deep blue sky was just like so many tiny insects. More secretive types of birds lived in the depth of the bush, and these were very beautiful, ranging in colour from a shimmering midnight blue to bright scarlet and molten gold. Unlike the chattering little dun-coloured fellows, they called to each other in soft low tones and, being curious about his footsteps, frequently flashed briefly on to the footpath ahead of him.

I wonder what the birds live on, he thought. The land on either side of the footpath was loose windblown sand and thornbush. Often the thornbush emerged as tall, straight-trunked trees, topped by an umbrella of black, exquisitely shaped branches, but more often it grew in short low tufts like rough wild grass. Long white thorns grew on the branches, at the base of which were tightly packed clusters of pale olive-green leaves. And that was all. As far as the eye could see it was only a vast expanse of sand and scrub but somehow bewitchingly beautiful. Perhaps he confused it with his own loneliness. Perhaps it was those crazy little birds. Perhaps it was the way the earth had adorned herself for a transient moment in a brief splurge of gold. Or perhaps he simply wanted a country to love and chose the first thing at hand. But whatever it was, he simply and silently decided that all this dryness and bleakness amounted to home and that somehow he had come to the end of a journey.

The little footpath spilled out suddenly on to a wide dirt road, and he had not walked far before a truck came lumbering up behind him. Like the gaudy-hued birds, the truck driver was curious about such an early traveller. He stopped the truck and called out, "Are you going to the station?"

"Yes," Makhaya said.

"It's always best to start early in the morning because the journey is long," the man said. "But you are lucky this time, I can give you a lift."

Later, he blessed the man silently. By truck it was a two-hour journey with not a hut or a living being in sight. On foot it might well have taken the whole day.

The only discomfort about the journey was that he had to invent lie after lie. The truck driver was talkative and kept on prying into his personal affairs.

"You've been to see relatives at the meraka?" the truck driver asked.

The word *meraka* was unknown to Makhaya, and it was only later that he was to learn that it was a cattle post. But he said, "Yes."

"And are they well?"

"No," he lied. "My mother is ill."

"Jo! And why doesn't she go into hospital?"

"She's a very stubborn old woman."

This seemed to be a huge joke to the truck driver. He laughed loudly. Then he said, "I see. You look like a teacher to me."

"I am," Makhaya lied again.

"In what village do you teach?"

"I'm not teaching at present. I've resigned to start a business."

The truck driver looked at him with interest. He half-averted his head, ill at ease. Should he tell the man he was a refugee? His experiences of the previous night had made him distrustful.

"I say," his questioner went on, "what's your tribe?"

He hesitated, trying to think of the nearest relationship to Zulus in the northern tribes. "Ndebele," he said.

"Don't be ashamed to mention it," the truck driver said sympathetically. "Foreigners are always welcome in our country."

And so it went on and on until Makhaya was exhausted from having to invent so many lies. He almost cried with relief when the truck-driver dropped him off at a railway crossing and continued on his journey to some unknown destination. Makhaya stood for a moment at the crossing to get his bearings. A sprawling village of mud huts was on one side of him and the railway station on the other. Clustered near the station were whatever brick buildings there were. It was a dismal-looking place and the brown dust of the dirt roads and footpaths was on everything. He was very hungry and stopped a passer-by and asked where he might buy some food. The man pointed to a filthy-looking restaurant which sold porridge and a plate of boiled meat for a shilling. A sign painted outside the dreadful eating house amused him. It said: HOTELA.

Because he had entered the country illegally he had to report to the police, register himself as a refugee, and apply for political asylum. Again, a passer-by pointed out the police station among the cluster of brick buildings. A British flag still flew above the small whitewashed building. The country was going through a year of self-government prior to complete independence. He stepped into a small office above which was written: STATION COMMANDER.

A British colonial police officer sat behind a desk on which was piled a jumble of papers. A notice on the wall above his head proclaimed: WORK FASCINATES ME. I CAN SIT AND WATCH IT FOR HOURS. He had quite a pleasant, good-looking face with arched eyebrows and green eyes. As commander of the station with no superior to jump to attention for, he exuded a great air of self-importance. He stared impassively at Makhaya for some time, then he said, "So you have come?"

Makhaya could make nothing of this remark and kept quiet.

"It's past eleven o'clock and I've delayed my tea waiting for you," he said. "In fact, I was just about to come and pick you up. Sit down, Mr. Makhaya Maseko."

"How do you know my name?" Makhaya asked, startled.

"I know everything," he said coolly. "I also want to impress you, so that you don't start any of your funny tricks around here. You may think this country is a backwater, but we have the most efficient intelligence service in southern Africa. We also read the newspapers."

He bent down and picked up a newspaper that had been carelessly flung on the floor. Makhaya's picture was on the front page under a headline: DANGEROUS SABOTEUR FLEES BANNING ORDER.

"I'm not dangerous and I'm not a saboteur," he said, annoyed.

"I know," the officer said. "You just dream about it. You just walk about with little pieces of paper describing how you're going to blow everything up."

He assumed a businesslike air searching among the jumble on his desk for a paper and pencil.

"You will have to answer a few routine questions," he said. He paused, then said, "Do you like Kwame Nkrumah?"

The complete unexpectedness of the question took Makhaya off guard and an automatic "No" slipped out before he had collected his wits. The officer grinned and relaxed into his casual manner.

"That's all," he said. "Fill in this form and you can go."

Makhaya sauntered out, uncertain of what to do next. Quite near the railway station was a post office. Around the post office was a fence, and an old man sat outside the fence, squatting very low on his haunches. He sat quite still, staring ahead with calm, empty eyes, and he looked so lordly for all his tattered coat and rough cowhide shoes that Makhaya smiled and walked up to him and greeted him. The old man withdrew his abstracted gaze and turned a pair of keen friendly eyes on Makhaya.

"You are a sociable man," he said, smiling. "Are you a stranger here?"

"Yes," Makhaya said and hesitated, not knowing what to say next.

The old man nodded his head as though he understood everything.

"Perhaps you are stranded?" he queried.

"Yes," Makhaya said again.

"But you look and sound like a well-educated man," he said in surprise.

Makhaya laughed. "Well-educated men often come to the crossroads of life," he said. "One road might lead to fame and importance, and another might lead to peace of mind. It's the road of peace of mind that I'm seeking."

The old man kept silent but he was thinking rapidly. The young man was very attractive, and he had a difficult daughter whom he wanted married before he died. The man's speech and ideas also appealed to him.

He said very carefully, "Most of the time we Batswana live in the wilderness and loneliness. We are used to it but I don't think you can stand it. Where do you come from?"

"South Africa," Makhaya said.

The old man shook his head. "That terrible place," he said. "The good God don't like it. This is God's country."

"God's country," Makhaya echoed, surprised.

"Didn't you know?" the old man said with a twinkle in his eye. "God is everywhere about here and it's no secret. People can't steal a thing from you, not even a sixpence. People can't fight, not even to kill an enemy."

Makhaya kept quiet, absorbing this strange philosophy. Everything about the old man pleased him, and noting this the old man said slyly, "Why not come and stay with me for a while, son."

"But I am almost penniless," Makhaya said.

"A poor person like me can still be hospitable," the old man said. "Besides, a lot is happening in my village and a well-educated man like you can bring a little light."

Chapter 2

The old man was not exaggerating when he said that a lot was happening in his village. Many factors had combined to make the village of Golema Mmidi a unique place. It was not a village in the usual meaning of being composed of large tribal or family groupings. Golema Mmidi consisted of individuals who had fled there to escape the tragedies of life. Its name too marked it out from the other villages, which were named after important chiefs or important events. Golema Mmidi acquired its name from the occupation the villagers followed, which was crop growing. It was one of the very few areas in the country where people were permanently settled on the land.

Normally, in other parts of the country, whole families would migrate in November to their lands on the outskirts of the villages to help with the ploughing and planting, returning to their villages in late January and leaving the June harvest to the women and children. Although people on the whole had to live off crops, they paid little attention to the land. The pivot of their lives was the villages. Not so with the people of Golema Mmidi. Necessity, even in some cases, rejection and dispossession in previous circumstances, had forced them to make the land the central part of their existence. Unlike the migratory villagers who set up crude, ram-shackle buildings on the edge of their lands, they built the large, wide, neatly thatched huts of permanent residence. They also had the best cultivated land and kept a constant watch on the thornbushes which sprang up in every conceivable place like weeds. True enough, the villagers did not differ so greatly from everyone else in their way of life.

The men attended to the cattle business and helped with the ploughing, while the women were the agriculturists or tillers of the earth. Like everyone else, they fenced their land with the thornbushes and supplemented their incomes with wood carving and basketmaking. A few like Makhaya's new-found companion, the old man, Dinorego, were skilled in the di-phate trade—that is, the making of mats and blankets from the skins of wild animals.

Over a period of fourteen years Golema Mmidi had acquired a population of four hundred people, and their permanent settlement there gave rise to small administrative problems. Due to this, a paramount chief named Sekoto had recognized it as a ward of his territory and for administrator had appointed his troublesome and unpopular younger brother, Matenge, as subchief of the village. The appointment took place in the sixth year of settlement, and although the residents politely addressed their subchief as "Chief", what had made Matenge unpopular in his brother's household—an overwhelming avariciousness and unpleasant personality—soon made him intensely disliked by the villagers, who were, after all, a wayward lot of misfits. Thus, appeal cases from Golema Mmidi were forever appearing on the court roll of the paramount chief—appeals against banishment, appeals against sentences for using threatening and insulting language to a subchief, and appeals against appropriation of property by the subchief. Knowing his brother well enough, the least the paramount chief could do was always to side with the appellants; and after a threat or two, the devil that drove Matenge would quickly subside, only to awaken its clamouring and howling a few months later.

One day, a strange, massively built, blue-eyed young man walked into the paramount chief's office.

He introduced himself as Gilbert Balfour and explained that he was but recently from England and had visited the country three years previously on a student's travel grant, and that to this visit he owed his choice of career—to assist in agricultural development and improved techniques of food production. The country presented overwhelming challenges, he said, not only because the rainfall was poor but because the majority of the people engaged in subsistence farming were using primitive techniques that ruined the land. All this had excited his interest. He had returned to England, taken a diploma in agriculture, and now had returned to Botswana to place his knowledge at the service of the country.

Then, for almost an hour he eagerly outlined a number of grand schemes, foremost of which was the role co-operatives could play in improving production and raising the standard of living. The paramount chief listened to it all with concealed alarm, though throughout the interview a smile of pleasant interest was on his face. Of course, he was widely known as a good chief, which is the way people usually refer to paramount chiefs. He attended all the funerals of the poor in the village, even accepted responsibility to bury those who were too poor to bury themselves, and had built a school here and a reservoir there. But because he was a chief he lived off the slave labour of the poor. His lands were ploughed free of charge by the poor, and he was washed, bathed, and fed by the poor, in return for which he handed out old clothes and maize rations. And to a man like this Gilbert Balfour came along and spent an hour outlining plans to uplift the poor! Most alarming of all, the Englishman had behind him the backing of a number of voluntary organizations who were prepared to finance his schemes at no cost to the country.

At first the young man's ideas caused the chief acute

discomfort, especially his habit of referring to the poor as though they were his blood brothers, and the chief was a shrewd enough judge of human nature to see that the young man was in deadly earnest. But halfway through the interview, a beaming smile lit up the chief's face. He would put this disturbing young man in Golema Mmidi, and if he could survive a year or more in the bedlam his brother Matenge would raise, that would be more than proof of his sincerity. One thing he was sure of—either the young man would be completely destroyed, or he would completely destroy his brother, and he wanted his brother destroyed for all the family feuds and intrigues he had instigated. Towards the end of the interview, he allocated a 250-acre plot for an experimental farm and a 7,000-acre plot for a cattle ranch.

It was about all this that the old man talked to Makhaya on their hour and a half walk to the village of Golema Mmidi. The village had no post office, and Dinorego had come to the railway village to take out some of his savings and purchase provisions that he could not buy in his village. When he had bought everything he needed, he put the provisions into a flour bag and slung it over his shoulder. The road they took ran parallel with the railway line, and once again it was just the thornbush on either side and the blue sky. Makhaya noticed that the old man had an odd way of walking. It was a quick shuffle, a propelled shuffle as though a small private windstorm was pushing him from behind, and his speech too had the odd propelled quality of his walk.

"It's not right," said Dinorego. "A well-educated man should not be stranded in our country. But you will find that things happen slowly here. They say this is a country where people ought not to live and it is true. Batswana people often go without food and water and so do their cattle. Cattle are grazed where a bit of grass grows, but water may only be found ten miles away. Life is like this: you graze cattle here one day; the next, you take them on a long search for water. It is such a hard life that I myself long ago gave up the cattle business. In all my years I have known of only one man who thinks he can change it. His name is Gilbert. He came to our village three years ago and started the cattle co-operative. Also a farm to try out better way of crop growing, and it is from this I mostly benefit as I only grow crops."

Dinorego stopped abruptly, put down his bundle and spread his hands out to explain himself more clearly. Makhaya listened in his absorbed, attentive way, a faint smile on his face.

"A Batswana man thinks like this: 'If there is a way to improve my life, I shall do it.' He may start by digging a well with a spade. He digs and digs, slowly moving the earth to one side with a spade. When it has become too deep, he sets up two poles in the earth with a pole on top and a handle. To this he attaches a rope and a bucket. Then he sends his son down into the well. The son digs and digs, each time sending up the earth in the bucket. At last water is found. Now, along comes someone and tells the man about rainwater dams that are made with scrapers. So the man inspans the oxen and makes a dam for watering his cattle by removing the earth with a scraper. That is how he progresses. Each time he feels he has improved himself a little, he is ready to try a new idea.

"In my village, people have long been ready to try out new ideas, but everything is delayed because of the fight that is going on between our chief and Gilbert. First of all the fight was about who is the good man and who is the evil man, though everyone well knows who the evil man is. In spite of this, many secret things were done to damage and delay the starting of the farm and cattle co-operative. Last year the secrets all came out into the open in the battle over Pelotona, the permit man. It is the rule that a permit must be written out for every beast that is sold. Before Gilbert came, Pelotona used to work for the chief because he was the big cattle speculator of the village. A cattle speculator works like this: a man brings his beast to him which he looks over and then says, 'Oh, I shall pay you six pounds for that beast.' But in his heart he knows he will get sixteen or twenty pounds for the same beast at the abattoir. This is the only way that a poor man may sell cattle because he cannot order railway trucks to transport his cattle. On this business our chief became very rich, then along came Gilbert with a new idea: the cattle co-operative belongs to the people and each member is to get a fair price. To get this fair price each beast is weighed on a scale and the owner is paid the same live weight as would be given by the abattoir. Seeing this good fortune, the whole village joined the cattle co-operative, putting our chief out of business.

"Now, Pelotona is a free man. He had a change of mind and walked over to work for Gilbert. The next thing our chief placed a banishment order on Pelotona, which made Pelotona straight-away run to our chief's brother Sekoto, who is also his superior. The chief's brother came over and said, 'You need not think because you are my relative that you can do what you like.' People were also much surprised to see a white woman come over from England and say in a very loud voice: 'Pelotona stays right here. We are paying his salary.' All this commotion over a poor and humble man like Pelotona."

There was a short silence. Makhaya was very moved by the vividly told little story, and there was the kind of defiance in the man Gilbert that found an echo in his own heart.

"Tell me more about Gilbert," he said quietly. "He interests me."

"I have no words to describe Gilbert, son," Dinorego said. "Just as I take you as my own son, so do I take Gilbert as my own son, which fact surprises me, since he is a white man and we Batswanas do not know any white people, though some have lived here for many years. Many things caused me to have a change of mind. He can eat goat meat and sour-milk porridge, which I have not known a white man to eat before. Also, whenever there is trouble he comes to me and says, 'Dinorego, should I stay here?' which fills my heart with fire since I am just an old man with no power. I reasoned: If Gilbert goes, who will pour out knowledge like rain? Everybody is selfish and wants to keep what he has to himself. There was my friend, Mma-Millipede, who had fifty-two fowls. They were wandering free, being eaten by the eagles. I took her myself to Gilbert. He says, 'If you have fifty-two fowls you must build a coop, fifteen feet by twenty-five feet. Make it six feet high. Keep one cockerel for every fifteen hens. Never keep more than two or three broody hens in the coop at one time. Buy egg-laying mash . . .' and so on. Mma-Millipede now always has eggs for sale."

The old man was silent awhile, then continued, "In this world are born both evil and good men. Both have to do justice to their cause. In this country there is a great tolerance of evil. It is because of death that we tolerate evil. All meet death in the end, and because of death we make allowance for evil though we do not like it."

"I might like it here," Makhaya said, wistfully.

"This country appeals to few people," said Dinorego. "There is too much loneliness. I stay alone with my youngest child. Her name is Maria. She likes all things modern. Because of this she is also taking lessons from Gilbert in English. One day she was looking at pictures in a book which Gilbert gave her.

There was a kitchen with shelves. So she carved the shelves in the mud wall. Then too, she cooks goat meat with curry powder and this improves its taste. Now all the women round about have shelves in their kitchens and cook the meat with curry powder."

There was an abrupt change in the scenery. The low wild thornbush suddenly gave way to acres and acres of cleared land, cultivated for ploughing. Perching on the outer borders of each plot were small groups of mud huts. At a railway siding, they crossed over the line and walked along a wide path that had been scraped by a bulldozer. The pathway wound and curved into the distance, and in the distance two low blue hills met and swept down to each other. At a fork in the road, a few tall, slender trees lined the pathway. Dinorego took the turning to the left.

"If you follow the other road," Dinorego said, "you will soon come to the farm and cattle co-operative. This is our village. It is called Golema Mmidi, which means 'to grow crops'."

A narrow footpath led through the trees which were planted by the old man on a slope that led down to his home. The short walk through the trees made Makhaya feel that the sudden clearing ahead of ploughed land was immense. Three huts stood nearby in a wide yard hedged with thornbush.

A young woman bent over sweeping the yard with a grass broom.

"Maria," the old man called. "I have a guest."

Those were familiar words to the young woman. Her father never seemed able to step out of his own village without bringing back a stranger. She straightened her back, glanced briefly at the tall stranger, and noticed immediately that he had the tired look of one who had travelled a long distance.

Perhaps he will want some water to wash, she

thought. It's a good thing I kept the big water pot near the fire.

She dropped the broom and walked quickly to one of the central huts and came out with two hand-carved stools which she placed on the ground for the men to sit on. Dinorego introduced her to Makhaya. She bent her knees in a slight curtsy and clasped two small hands together in the Tswana form of greeting.

"Tea will soon be ready," she said. "Would the guest like water to wash?"

It was the crisp clear voice of a busy, preoccupied, self-absorbed woman, and there was an almighty air of neatness and orderliness about her. She was very thin with a long pretty neck on which was poised a serious, quiet face, and her small black eyes never seemed to gaze outward, but inward. In fact, she was often in the habit of staring meditatively at the ground. Makhaya was instantly attracted to her.

Thunderous footsteps made Makhaya swing sharply around. This made the old man laugh.

"It's Gilbert," he said. "He always surprises people because no one expects such a big man."

He was not big, he was a giant, and his massive frame made him topple forward slightly and sway as he walked. He never wore much except short khaki pants and great hobnailed boots, and because of this, the sun had burned him a dark brown hue, and this in turn accentuated the light-blue colouring of his eyes so that they glittered. Life never seemed to offer enough work for his abundant energy, and his gaze forever restlessly swept the horizon seeking some new challenge, while at the same time his mind and hands could busy themselves with the most immediate and insignificant details in a continuous flow of activity like a wave. Thus, having already included Makhaya and Dinorego in his horizon, he walked straight into the central hut, said something that made Maria laugh, and came out almost immediately with a stool and the tea tray.

"Dinorego," he said, pleasantly. "Why didn't you tell me you were going into town? I could have given you a lift, as I wanted to go in too to buy a new mantle for my lamp."

"It's a good thing I did not ask for a lift, Gilbert," the old man said. "Today I was meant to acquire a new son. His name is Makhaya."

Gilbert held out his hand and smiled widely, easily. "Hullo, Mack . . ." he stumbled as he had not really grasped the sound of it.

"It's just a tribal name," Makhaya said, smiling at his embarrassment. "You can call me Mack if you like."

The words, "It's just a tribal name," caused an instant pause in the activity of the wave. To Gilbert, it was the first real handclasp he had experienced in the loneliness in which he found himself in tribal Africa. He stared at Makhaya, taking in the quiet, wryly amused expression and the air of lonely self-containment.

"Are you a stranger to this country?" he asked.

"Yes," Makhaya said, then added, "I also ought to be passing through because I'm a refugee."

"To where?" Gilbert asked.

"I don't know yet," Makhaya said.

Gilbert said nothing, yet the expression on his face went blank the way it always did when someone aroused sympathy in him.

Maria came up and said very formally to Makhaya, "Sir, the water for your wash is ready."

Makhaya picked up his bag and followed her to one of the huts. Gilbert turned to Dinorego and said, "He's quite a strange fellow."

"Not only that, Gilbert," the old man said quickly. "He has some wonderful ideas. When I first met him he said 'A man comes to the crossroads. The one road leads to fame and the other to peace of mind. Is there peace of mind for a man like me?' And I straight away thought: 'This is the very man my son Gilbert has been looking for to help him in his work. Since he is a well-educated man perhaps they can have some understanding.' What do you think?"

He blinked innocently at Gilbert.

Gilbert kept quiet for a moment, then said, decisively, "I'll invite him to have supper with me."

Gilbert gazed thoughtfully into the distance. The quietly amused words, "It's just a tribal name," kept on recurring to him. He needed, more than anything, someone with the necessary mental and emotional alienation from tribalism to help him accomplish what he had in mind. Three years of uphill battling had already made clear to him his own limitations in putting his ideas across to people, and he had also learned that change, if it was to take place at all, would in some way have to follow the natural course of people's lives rather than impose itself in a sudden and dramatic way from on top. He hadn't the kind of personality that could handle people, because everything in him was submerged to the work he was doing. He lacked sympathy, patience and understanding, and there were all those weird conflicts he had had with Matenge that had kept him lying awake at night. There seemed to be no escape from the man, but what had contributed more than anything else to those sleepless nights was his own inability to understand the workings of an extremely cunning and evil mind, a mind so profoundly clever as to make the innocent believe they were responsible for the evil.

As soon as Makhaya emerged from the hut, Gilbert stood up and said abruptly, "Would you care to have supper with me? I'd like to talk to you."

Gilbert led the way out of the yard, up the slope and through the trees. A flock of goats suddenly appeared, herded home by a small boy. The sun had already set, and as though they knew this, the goats flicked their tails briskly and rolled anxious yellow eyes at the two men watching them as much as to say: "We are late, but one day we will stop and talk." The small boy waved, walking in the same manner as the briskly trotting goats.

As though he understood goat-talk, Gilbert laughed happily. He said to Makhaya, "Botswana goats amaze me. They just walk about eating all this dry paper and bits of rubble and then turn it into meat and milk."

They walked on and soon came to the wide pathway which forked with a turning to the left and one to the right: Gilbert took the turn to the right and they arrived at a big gate, roughly made of tautly strung barbed wire. Gilbert lifted the wire latch and swung the gate open, and then closed it again once Makhaya was inside. He raised one hand and said gaily:

"This is Utopia, Mack. I've the greatest dreams about it."

And all that Makhaya could see of Utopia in the dimming light was the outline of several mud huts. Near one of these was parked a Land-Rover and to this hut Gilbert walked. He pushed open the door and struck a match to light a lamp. The interior was simply furnished with a bed in one corner, a table, two chairs and some boxes on which were strewn, in haphazard order, books and magazines. Makhaya sat down on one of the chairs while Gilbert pumped a paraffin stove which stood on the floor in a corner of the hut. Supper was to be a few tins of canned food emptied into a pot and heated briefly over the stove and then poured out roughly on to two plates. But while he busied himself, Gilbert chatted about this and that.

"I like it here," he said. "I'm running away from England. You know what England's like? It's full of nice, orderly queues, and everybody lines up in these queues for a place and position in the world. I let all that go hang and hopped out."

He paused and looked at Makhaya with a friendly glance. "What exactly are you running away from?"

"It's not so much what I'm running away from," Makhaya said. "It's what I'm trying to run into. I want a wife and children."

Gilbert looked half-surprised and half-amused at this unexpected reply.

Makhaya laughed. "I want some part of myself to go on when I die," he said. "And since I found myself so near death over the past two years, I thought it best to find a wife before I found anything else."

"Are you that simple?" Gilbert asked, and laughed too.

"Yes," Makhaya said.

"I don't know if the same applies to me," Gilbert said, suddenly thoughtful. "Ninety per cent of the time I don't want a woman. Then also there's that ten per cent when I'm lonely, but I don't know of any woman who'd go for the ten per cent."

"She would," Makhaya said. "But provided she had a life of her own too."

Gilbert looked at him with an almost childlike innocence. "You seem to be quite an expert."

Makhaya averted his face in discomfort. He could not explain that experiences went hand in hand with a depth of bitterness and resentment because he did not fully understand the root cause of an attraction that had made women pursue him; that if love was basically a warm fire in you, you attracted all the cold people who consumed your fire with savage greed leaving you deprived and desolate. The robbery he recognized but not the cause.

"I have sisters," Makhaya said at last. "Also, there have been women and women in my life, I suppose because I searched for them."

They were silent for a while, eating. Then Gilbert said quietly:

"Would you say, from what you've seen of her today, that Dinorego's daughter was one of those women who had a life of her own?"

Makhaya did not reply immediately. He thought of the small black inward-gazing eyes and the pretty air of preoccupied self-absorption. He'd have liked a woman like that. She might have so easily become a part of this inner harmony and peace he was striving for. But an instinct warned him to push the dream away from him. Three years was a long time and he was a stranger to it all.

"Yes," he said, slowly. "I'd say she's that kind of woman."

Gilbert's eyes lit up with laughter. "She's hard to get," he said. "She makes all these little rules and you can't budge her from them. When I first came here I asked her to marry me and she said, 'I can't marry you, Gilbert, because I'm not an educated woman. You won't be happy with an uneducated woman.' So I said, 'All right, get educated then.' Now I'm sorry I ever said it because I've been teaching her English in exchange for lessons in Tswana. All I've got out of it is an inferiority complex over my inability to grasp Tswana."

This odd little confession warmed Makhaya's heart to the man. There might have been so many things that could have stood up as a barrier between a possible friendship, like Makhaya's background and his distrust and dislike of white people. Instead, he found himself confronted by a big man who allowed himself to be bullied by a small woman. They sat in companionable silence for a while, then Gilbert stood up and cleared away the plates and crouched down on one knee, pretending to fuss about putting them in a basin. He half-turned and looked at Makhaya.

"I could do with a friend around here," he said, slightly embarrassed. "Are you looking for a job?"

"Yes," Makhaya said.

"Tell me a bit about yourself. What work were you doing in South Africa?"

"There's not much to tell," Makhaya said. "I worked for a newspaper in Johannesburg. It was the only sort of thing where black people could see their faces on the front page and read about their neighbours, but it was lurid. And since I went out on the stories I could see that it was not so far from the truth because people who are down in the hovels are lurid. The only thing is, it's a law of life that they rise up but there are man-made laws to keep them down there. After a time it begins to drive you crazy. You either drink too much, or you join underground sabotage movements which are riddled with spies. You keep a piece of paper in your pocket with a plan to blow something up, and you get thrown into jail for two years before you've blown anything up."

"Do you still feel committed to all this?" Gilbert asked.

"Wouldn't I have stayed there if I had?" Makhaya said, half-questioning himself. "I don't know. Nothing is quite clear to me."

Gilbert stood up and swung around decisively. "Can you drive a car?" he asked.

"Yes," Makhaya said.

"Driving a tractor is much easier," he said. "Part of your job would be to learn tractor ploughing and the use of planters, harrows, and cultivators. The other half would be to teach women agriculture."

Makhaya stared at him in amazement. "But I know nothing about agriculture," he protested.

"I have the lectures," Gilbert said, almost impatiently. "I know what's needed but I can't teach. I can't put my ideas over somehow, and not only because my grasp of Tswana is poor."

He sat down on the chair and for almost an hour talked eagerly, the way he had with the paramount chief, only this time to a keenly attentive listener.

He felt that he had stumbled on to one of the major blockages to agricultural progress in the country. The women were the traditional tillers of the earth, not the men. The women were the backbone of agriculture while the men on the whole were cattle drovers. But when it came to programmes for improved techniques in agriculture, soil conservation, the use of pesticides and fertilizers, and the production of cash crops, the lecture rooms were open to men only. Why give training to a section of the population who may never use it but continue to leave it to their wives to erode the soil by unsound agricultural practices? Why start talking about development and food production without taking into account who is really producing the food?

At each turn he had been struck by the complexity of the structure. Golema Mmidi was, for most of the year, a village of women with all the men away at the cattle posts. Dinorego was the only full-time male crop producer in the village. All the rest were women. What Gilbert had in mind was to bring the two, cattle production and crop production, together. The system of uncontrolled grazing far out in the bush, apart from ruining the land, was only producing low-grade beef. If cattle were brought to the crop-producing areas, they could be fed on the crop residues and grain surpluses, and this would raise the grade of the beef. There was a serious reason for finding urgent solutions. The country was in the grip of a severe drought, which had already lasted five years and was becoming worse with each succeeding year.

"Well, Mack, what do you think?" he said at last.

Makhaya spread out his hands, helplessly. It was a whole new, astonishing world.

"I think I'll accept the job," he said.

"You can move in tonight," Gilbert said.

He picked up the lamp and led the way to a nearby hut which was furnished on the same lines as his own. Then they walked to the home of Dinorego to fetch Makhaya's baggage. The old man's heart was full of joy. He thought he had indeed acquired a son in Makhaya. Once the two young men's footsteps had retreated out of sound, he turned to his daughter and said, "Well, what do you think of the stranger, my child?"

"He's all right," Maria replied, with profound indifference.

She stood up from her place at the fire and went to bed. The old man sat for a long while contemplating the flames. Would he see no grandchildren? Would Maria never love a man?

Chapter 3

Not anything in his life had prepared Makhaya for his first week in his new employment. There was so much that excited the interest of Gilbert about the country, and he was anxious to impart three years of observation all at once to Makhaya to give him a base on which to work.

Golema Mmidi was in the eastern part of the country, in a watershed area that received an average annual rainfall of eighteen inches, while vast stretches of the western region were almost desert and received an average annual rainfall of nine inches. Thus, the eastern watershed was also the most heavily over-stocked and overgrazed and overpopulated part of the country. Because of this, much of the softer, sweeter types of grass had long since disappeared from the area, and great stretches of land were covered by a species known as the carrot-seed grass. This was a tough, quick-growing little annual. Its short impoverished leaves grew close to the ground in a spread-out, star-shaped pattern from the centre of which arose a thin stalk, profusely covered by close-packed little burrs. These burr grass seeds clung to the mouth parts and legs of the animals and were so transported from place to place.

The carrot-seed grass grew in profusion all over Golema Mmidi. When Gilbert first arrived and fenced in the 250-acre plot for cultivation, he had left a wide strip of land between the fence and the cultivated area. At first, on this border strip, the carrot-seed grass grew.

Over a period of two rainy seasons, a number of interesting changes took place on this border strip.

Springing up between the carrot-seed during the first season were the long frail, feathery stalks of the wind-blown eragrostis, a lush sweet grass. Within two years, this type of grass had gained dominion over the border strip area, crowding out the carrot-seed grass, which by then had ceased to grow. This amazing development caused Gilbert to place the carrot-seed under closer observation in a rough, home-made laboratory. He noted that carrot-seed showed a preference for impoverished soil, but once the burr casing had liberated the tiny seed, it rotted, forming a humus layer in the soil. Thus, while not liking rich soil, it had the ability to build up the humus layer in impoverished soil and was the tough pioneer which paved the way for a more fragile species of grass to gain its hold on the soil again.

Other miracles too had taken place in the border strip. The minute star faces of wild flowers peeked up amidst the now dense grass: white stars and purple stars and the lacy curving sprays of delicate blends of pale-pink blossoms with, here and there, the jaunty yellow-gold of strange freakish daisies with stems that were one inch wide and flat as rulers, topped by flowers with the odd shape of inverted whorls. A strange gourd too crept along the fence, the hard outer husk of the fruit enclosing enormous seeds which were covered by a thin film of syrup that tasted like honey.

Had all this strange new growth lain dormant for years and years in the soil? He questioned the villagers, but only Dinorega, one of the earliest settlers, retained a wistful memory of when the whole area had been clothed by waist-high grass and clear little streams had flowed all the year round. The pathways of the streams were still there but dry and empty now.

Gilbert travelled all over the eastern watershed area and in dismay often came upon abandoned villages that had been turned into sandy wastelands through the grazing of the cattle and the goats. In some of these wastelands even the carrot-seed grass had completely died out, and the only type of vegetation that held the soil together was the thornbush. These observations convinced him that only large-scale fencing of the land and controlled grazing would save the parts that had not yet become completely eroded and uninhabitable to both man and animals. But it was his enthusiasm for fencing and his criticism of the tribal land tenure system that first brought him to a head-on clash with the fuming Chief Matenge.

Not fully understanding the complexity of the land tenure system, Gilbert had announced that it was a hindrance to agricultural progress. Matenge's brother, the paramount chief, had broken precedent when he allowed Gilbert to fence the land. Fencing of tribal land was not allowed, as ownership of the land was vested in the tribe as a whole. No man could claim that he had purchased a plot of tribal land and anyone who asked was merely allocated a portion free of charge by a chief. This system was designed to protect the interests of the poor and to prevent the land from falling into the hands of a few rich people. Intent on his own schemes for reclaiming eroded soil, Gilbert was shocked to discover that he was the centre of a violent storm. Chief Matenge, aware that he was about to lose his lucrative cattle-dealing business with the villagers, grabbed on the fencing of the farm and cattle ranch to convince the villagers of Gilbert's evil intentions towards them. In alarm, the villagers called a meeting and sent a deputation of old men to Gilbert.

Was it true, they wanted to know, that Gilbert had in reality secretly purchased land from the paramount chief and was using the name of co-operative to enslave the people? That was what Chief Matenge had told them. At first Gilbert was dumbstruck by the accusation. Then he realized that he had endangered his work by criticizing the land system and creating the impression that he favoured freehold tenure.

No, Gilbert had replied, he was not proposing an alternative to the tribal land tenure system. He believed that co-operative organization was similar to communal ownership of land, and he felt that progress could be achieved if enclosed grazing land, farm machinery, boreholes, and marketing societies were the responsibility of the members.

Dinorego, who had acted as interpreter of the deputation, pointed to the fences. Why had barbed-wire fencing been set up around the land? It was something that was not allowed. They did not doubt the word of the young man, he said kindly, but all the commotion was over the fences.

Gilbert took them to the border strip area to show them how good grass regained its hold on the land once the earth was protected by a fence. All the old men could not but agree that they had not seen such grass in Golema Mmidi for a long time. He also took them to the cattle ranch where the same miracle had occurred. The cattle ranch had been divided into four camps. Two were to remain empty for some time. In one of the empty camps, he wished to observe the speed with which the natural grasses of the area recovered. In the other he had had the land de-stumped and ploughed and a drought-resistant type of grass seed sown. From this he would be able to judge whether indigenous grasses or imported drought-resistant grasses would be best suited for cattle grazing.

In the two occupied camps he had retained one hundred cattle which he had purchased from the co-operative members. The best of these were to be used in a stock-breeding experiment, and these would then be resold to members wishing to restock their herds.

The last camp was also an experiment to raise the grade of the meat. The cattle of camp number four were fed on a special type of corn that produced only stems and leaves and was grown on the farm as part of the year's crop. Water, bonemeal, and salt licks were also provided within the fenced-off area of this camp.

Gilbert explained that without fencing he could not gather all this valuable information. Also, it was his hope that all the cattle of Golema Mmidi would one day graze on co-operatively owned feeding grounds, and the fencing of these feeding grounds was most essential for a number of reasons. There could be no overstocking once a fence was erected. The plan was to keep no more than two hundred cattle at a time on a ranch of seven thousand acres. If fewer beasts were kept, they could be better fed, and this would bring an increase in their cash value. Fencing also reduced the hardship and labour of cattle-rearing. No longer would cattle stray and get lost in the bush, and it prevented the spread of infectious diseases like foot-and-mouth.

The old men were deeply impressed. They all were or had been cattlemen and immediately grasped the significance of what they saw and heard. The young man's entry into their village had not gone unnoticed, nor had his deeds or his ability, though educated, to live under the same conditions as the poor. But the deputation was concerned about the young man's truthfulness and sincerity, for everyone from the chiefs down to the colonial authorities had lived off the poor in one form or another and in the name of one thing or another, like cow tax, hut tax, manhood tax, and tax on not paying manhood tax. Gilbert gained two advantages out of this meeting with the old men of the village: the establishment of the co-operative movement in Golema Mmidi and the friendship of Dinorego.

Out of the two, it was difficult to say which he valued more. Without the villagers' enthusiasm for co-operatives, his dreams would have remained at a standstill. Yet without the friendship of Dinorego he might not have survived the frustrations of three years and the continual enmity of Chief Matenge.

Progress was slow. The main purpose of the 250-acre plot was to try and prove whether, if run with modern machinery, it could win crops under all but the most severe drought conditions. Yet he was under pressure to make the farm economically viable; he had established it on grants and donations which would not continue indefinitely. The distractions were immense. The drought became worse with each succeeding year, and the rainfall pattern became exceedingly unpredictable. At times a whole year's rain might fall in one month or one day or one hour. For the past two years, few of the villagers had reaped an adequate amount of crops.

When he first arrived in Golema Mmidi, all the ploughing was done by oxen, and these were always in a weak condition by the time the first rains fell. Almost six weeks of the rainy season had to pass by before the oxen, fed on the fresh green growth, were strong enough to plough. In the meanwhile, all the good rain needed by the crops might fall in those six weeks. This created anxiety, and often a man would harness his plough team too soon, only to have them topple over from weakness created by the long walks in search of the scant grazing during the dry season.

Gilbert's solution of this predicament was a thrift and loan club which enabled the villagers to hire machinery from the farm so that they could take immediate advantage of any rainfall. Most of the men of the village had taken their first lessons in tractor-ploughing at the farm.

All this covered the range of his achievements so

far, yet these achievements seemed to him very unsatisfactory. Apart from growing crops for food, crops that brought in cash had to be grown too. This called for trying out new ways of making the land produce all the crops a man might need to support his life. His views reached out to no one but Dinorego. Gilbert was to find that strange prejudices surrounded people's eating habits and the types of crops they were prepared to grow.

He had approached the authorities to inquire as to the amount of research that was being done in the country on breeding drought-resistant strains of seed. He found out that the most intensive research had been done on millet. Millet was really a stranger to southern Africa where sorghum and maize are eaten as a daily staple. Yet fifteen thousand varieties of millet had been tested in the country, and the authorities had finally bred a type that could produce a crop in only three inches of rain, with a few most needed advantages. Witchweed, which is a parasite that is germinated by and lives on the roots of maize and sorghum plants, stunting their growth, was germinated by this type of millet as well, yet the plant remained unaffected by it. Also, the red-billed weaver bird that lives off sorghum seed and caused heavy damage to crops each year, bypassed the millet because the ear produced a lot of spiky hairs that irritated the throat of the bird.

"So everybody is growing millet?" Gilbert queried the authorities.

"No," they said. "Everybody is still growing sorghum and maize."

He looked at them dumbfounded. Were they deliberately sitting on research information? And they merely laughed at his look of baffled surprise.

They also shrugged. They had done their best to publicize the millet discovery, and what had happened? Countries at the ends of the earth had grabbed it, but the discovery had made no impact on Botswana because certain minority tribes, traditionally considered inferior, had long had a liking for millet and had always grown it as part of the season's crop. Therefore, other tribes who considered themselves superior would not grow it nor eat it. These "inferior" tribes lived in the wastes of the Kalahari Desert where the rainfall barely averaged nine inches a year, and it was their success in growing millet under such conditions that had first aroused interest in millet breeding. But the agricultural authorities decided it wasn't the policy of their department to interfere with the traditional prejudices of the Batswana people.

"But why don't you tell people that millet is a cash crop?" Gilbert said, hotly. "Why don't you say, 'If you don't want to eat it, grow it and market it. Grow it and make this the greatest millet-producing country in the world because it's the one kind of crop that's certain to do well here.'"

They shrugged again. "Can't people reason things out for themselves?" they said.

He looked at them appalled. So that's what colonial authority amounted to? Do your bit and the job was done. He bought the millet seed and walked out. One day, these colonial authorities were so unfortunate as to pick up a rumour that all was not well with Gilbert in the village of Golema Mmidi. They wrote him a pally letter: "Why not come and join us, old boy?" He sent back an unprintable reply.

It was Dinorego who confirmed the story of the authorities. It was true, he said. Millet was only grown and eaten by "inferior" tribes. But once Gilbert grew it on the farm as a cash crop, Dinorego quickly followed suit and grew it on his own land.

Drought-resistant breeds of maize and sorghum,

which more people in Botswana were prepared to eat, were hard to find. There was a certain species of slightly drought-resistant sorghum, but this species produced a layer of black substance just under the outer husk, and when pounded and cooked, it made the porridge look black in colour. For this reason it was unpopular and never grown.

Year in and year out people had grown the exact same crops. Somewhere along the line they had become mixed up with tribal traditions. They had become fixed. They were: Sorghum, maize, watermelon, and sweet reed. There was even a feeling of safety about them. Never mind if the hot sun of the drought years burned whole fields of sorghum and maize. Never mind if the rain was no longer what it used to be in the good old days when the rivers ran the whole year round and the dams were always full. You just could not see beyond tradition and its safety to the amazing truth you were starving—and that tough little plants existed that were easy to grow and well able to stand up to rigorous conditions and could provide you with food.

How could a start be made? How could people and knowledge be brought together? Could the women of the village be given some instruction? And why not? Women were on the land 365 days of the year while the men shuttled to and fro with the cattle. Perhaps all change in the long run would depend on the women of the country and perhaps they too could provide a number of solutions to problems he had not yet thought of. Things could start in a small way with crops like millet, with talks, with simple lectures, and with some practical work done on the land.

Gilbert had drawn up a broad rough outline of his plans for instructing women, and this he handed to Makhaya to study. Makhaya in turn had a mind like a sponge. It soaked up knowledge. By the end of one week he had fully grasped the background against which he was to work. Strange as agriculture might have been to him a week previously, he settled down quite happily with books on soil conservation and tractor-ploughing, and catalogues of wild veld grasses. He was quite unaware that while he sat up reading at night, Chief Matenge was losing a considerable amount of sleep over his presence in the village and his employment at the farm.

Chief Matenge lived in the central part of the village in a big cream-painted mansion. He had once been married and divorced, his wife retaining the two children of the marriage. For many years he had lived alone in the cream mansion until quite recently he had acquired a guest and friend in a certain politician named Joas Tsepe. The central part of the village was about two miles from the farm and it contained, apart from Matenge's mansion, one very poor General Dealer's shop, which supplied the villagers with only the bare necessities like sugar, tea, flour and vegetable fats, and cheap materials and shoes; one three-roomed shack, which was the village primary school; and a square brick building that was the depot for collecting and distributing mail from the post office of the railway village, twenty miles away. Mail was received and distributed once a week at this depot. A group of mud huts clustered about the cream-painted mansion, and in these mud huts the servants of Matenge lived, not servants in the ordinary sense, because they were paid no wage, but slaves he had received as part of his heritage.

The mansion, the slaves, and a huge cream Chevrolet, which he parked under a tree in the yard, were the only things that gave Matenge a feeling of security in the village. At least this part of it was in order. The chiefs had always lived in the mansions while the people had lived in the huts. His world had always known two strict classes: royalty and commoner. Golema Mmidi was a village of commoners. Not one could claim even distant relationship to royalty and dispute his authority, and the old men whom he had elected as advisers on village affairs were not so much advisers as messenger-boys who had to transmit his deeply resented orders to the villagers. True enough, there was Mma-Millipede, a commoner, who had once been married to the son of a chief. But she was also a rejected woman and, in his eyes, a degraded woman. He was aware of her popularity in the village and that people often consulted her, but after investigations he found out that this was only because of respect for her religious views, and she no longer troubled him. The villages were full of such cranky old women with a bit of missionary education and the Tswana version of the Bible.

Still, he felt insecure. He should have reigned supreme over the commoners, and yet his eight-year administration of the village had dealt one shattering blow after another to his self-esteem. It was he who displayed the arrogance and pride that were part and parcel of the bearing of a great chief, and yet life had placed an amiable, pleasant nitwit of a brother in the supreme position, who was not above shaking hands with the commoners and talking to them as equals. It was he, Matenge, who really commanded the largest following of diehard traditionalists, the ones who from generation to generation saw to it that things remained as they were and whose company and advice were anathema to his carefree, pleasure-loving elder brother, the paramount chief. It was he, Matenge, who understood tribalism, that it was essentially the rule of the illiterate man who, when he was in the majority, feared and despised anything that was not a part of the abysmal darkness in which he lived. (Matenge was the epitome of this darkness with his long, gloomy, melancholy, suspicious face and his ceaseless intrigues, bitter jealousy and hatred.) All this was tribalism and a way of life to the meek sheep who submitted to it. And all this had been highly praised by the colonialists as the only system that would keep the fearful, unwieldly, incomprehensible population of "natives" in its place.

And yet, things were changing rapidly. The colonialists were withdrawing, and the change was not so much a part of the fashionable political ideologies of the New Africa as the outcome of the natural growth of a people. Matenge could not see this. His brother the paramount chief could, and swam with the outgoing tide, enjoying himself the meanwhile. Matenge could not see this because it had always been his policy to transfer hate from one object to another, and if at last he found himself involved in the political ideologies of Africa and the cauldron of hatred, it was because it was the last camp that reflected his traditional views.

At first Matenge had hated his brother because he felt the chieftaincy should be his, and this hatred drove him to overreach himself until he was discovered in a plot to assassinate his brother. For this his brother smilingly and politely banished him to Golema Mmidi under the guise that he was being given an administrative post. The shock of it kept him quiet for some time, but soon he transferred his hate to the villagers, most notably Dinorego, who had refused to sit on his advisory council. For this he tried to get Dinorego banished from the area, but the banishment order was immediately rescinded by his brother. And so it had gone on. The villagers were aware of the tug of war, but they feared Matenge too much to take open advantage of it. They merely avoided him as much as possible. Then, along had come Gilbert Balfour, who, with his brother's backing, destroyed Matenge's lucrative cattle-speculating business overnight. The hatred, which had by now become a mountain, was once more transferred to Gilbert. And if the times had not really changed he might have won this last battle and got Gilbert removed from the village by the colonial authorities.

Co-operatives were not a popular cause. The cattle-speculating monopolies were in the hands of a few white traders, but once the people had voted a government into power that gave its support to co-operatives, the traders had reacted in panic and started paying inflated prices for cattle. It all depended on how long they could hold out in competition against the co-operatives. Some people welcomed this development. The traders had become rich at the expense of the people, and now they were paying these same people fantastic sums of money for cattle. Surely that's the best way a greedy man may dig his own grave? In the meantime, a fierce battle raged and *co-operatives* was the dirtiest word you could use to the monopolists.

The agricultural authorities also believed they had a monopoly over the future development of the country, and they were not inclined to favour independent initiative, nor outsiders. Development was an "in" business, for locals only. They were prepared to welcome Gilbert "in", as he was a white man, but to their extreme chagrin, they found that he had independent ideas about that too.

It seemed impossible to Matenge that one man could stir up so much trouble among the important people and still remain in the country. And he kept the pot boiling all the time, in the hope that one side or the other would step in and rid him of his arch enemy.

Almost a week passed before Matenge became

aware of Makhaya's presence in the village and he got to know of it through the only friend he had, Joas Tsepe.

Joas Tsepe was the undersecretary general of the Botswana National Liberation Party. There were four or five such liberation parties with little or no membership among the people but many undersecretary generals. All these parties opposed the new government. At first, this opposition had set as its goal the liberation of the Botswana people from colonialism. But after the self-government elections, it forgot about the colonialists and set itself to liberate the Botswana people from a government they had elected into power. The opposition maintained that the people did not know what they were doing. They claimed that the colonialists had rigged the elections, although prior to the voting the opposition had anticipated this colonial treachery and had specially asked to be represented at the ballot counting table. Strangely enough, in front of their very eyes, power had passed into the hands of the ruling party. Strangely enough too, Joas and quite a few others of his clan served six-month sentences for rigging election papers. They also spent some time blowing hot air about the stupid Botswana people who had voted for chiefs and then, to their amazement, found that they had a government of the sons of chiefs with an anti-chief policy. Joas's party and the other opposition groups quickly reorganized themselves into pro-chief supporters, as the chiefs had by now become the only disgruntled section of the country.

The opposition political parties had long been aligned to the Pan-African movement. They also called themselves the vanguard of African nationalism in southern Africa. To many, Pan-Africanism is an almost sacred dream, but like all dreams it also has its nightmare side, and the little men like Joas Tsepe and their strange doings are the nightmare. If they have any power at all it is the power to plunge the African continent into an era of chaos and bloody murder.

Joas Tsepe, although born in Botswana, spent a number of years working in South Africa. There he also acquired a number of grievances, which even the whole world acknowledges as being justifiable. Having made a little reputation for himself as a speaker at political meetings, he was one day, from some mysterious source, given the order to go back to his country to fight for the liberation of his people. This mysterious source also supplied him with money which enabled him to remain unemployed and devote himself full-time to the liberatory struggle, and also to purchase a car. Every six months, he left the country "on a mission", for which mission he was supplied with an air ticket to travel to various parts of the earth.

All this VIP treatment gave Joas a swollen head. He was already the minister of finance in the shadow government, and this caused one to pause and puzzle out the motives of the financier of his mysterious source of money, since Joas was ill-equipped educationally to handle the complicated business of government, and a course in economics would have been far better than the VIP trips. Was it perhaps the intention of the secret financier to reestablish the rule of the illiterate and semi-literate man in Africa? Or was Joas his tool? Was it easier for a man like Joas to take his orders? Because Joas was a parrot. Not only that, he was a belly-crawler and it was his agility at belly-crawling that had won him the friendship of Matenge. Since he had come out of jail after the self-government elections, Joas lived as the permanent guest of Matenge. He had a co-operative to organize which would help Matenge to re-establish himself as the cattle-speculator of Golema Mmidi, and he had to educate the African masses in African socialism.

It was on Friday afternoon that Joas passed by the farm and noticed the presence of a stranger. Devoured by curiosity, he swung into the farm gates on the plea that he needed water for a long journey. He took one close look at Makhaya and almost choked with excitement. The newspaper with Makhaya's picture on the front page was in his car, and his car could not seem to drive fast enough back to Matenge.

He burst in on Matenge, waving the paper. "We've got him this time, Chief," he said, dramatically.

Matenge looked bored. That was the way a superior had to behave to an inferior. Getting no response, Joas opened the paper and held it before Matenge.

"Gilbert is keeping a refugee at the farm," he said.

The whole weekend Matenge stewed and simmered. Gilbert had overshot himself. If there was anything the new government disliked, it was a refugee, and because of this, no man in his right senses would harbour or employ one. Early Monday morning, Matenge climbed into his cream Chevrolet and drove to the village of his brother, Paramount Chief Sekoto.

Chapter

Even those who did not like chiefs had to concede that Paramount Chief Sekoto was a very charming man. His charm lay not so much in his outer appearance as in his very cheerful outlook on life. In fact, so fond was he of the sunny side of life that he was inclined to regard any gloomy, pessimistic person as insane and make every effort to avoid his company. It was his belief that a witty answer turneth away wrath and that the oil of reason should always be poured on troubled waters.

Chief Sekoto had three great loves: fast cars, good food, and pretty girls. All the good food had made him very fat, so that he gave the impression of waddling like a duck when he walked. And one of the pretty girls had caused a major disruption in his otherwise serene and happy life. It happened like this. About two miles from his official residence, he had built a palatial mansion. He had sternly forbidden his wife to set foot in this mansion on the grounds that it was here that he entertained important guests with whom he discussed top-secret affairs. But it wasn't long before the wife and the whole village knew that this was the house where Chief Sekoto kept his concubines. Still, not a murmur of protest was raised against him, it being taken for granted that a chief was entitled to privileges above those of ordinary men. For many years Chief Sekoto carefully divided his attention between his two homes until one day he chanced upon an exceedingly beautiful woman, lost his head, and for three months took up permanent residence in the mansion of the concubines. The villagers took it lightly. The scandal was huge entertainment in the humdrum round of their daily life. Not so for the chief's family.

Towards the end of the third month, Chief Sekoto was forced to take a long business trip. His absence from the village gave his family the opportunity to make short work of the troublesome concubine. The chief's eldest son drove up to the mansion, bundled the concubine roughly into a car, and sped with her out of the village to some unknown destination. Not only that, the foolhardy young man had an intense, upright character and quarreled violently with his amiable father and walked out of the house, forever. This experience was a great shock to Chief Sekoto. He knew in his heart that he would never give up the pretty girls, but after that he kept his hunting grounds well away from home.

Every weekday morning, Chief Sekoto listened to cases brought before his court, while the afternoons were spent at leisure unless there were people who had made appointments to interview him. This particular Monday morning a lively and rowdy case was in session when, out of the corner of his eye, Chief Sekoto saw his brother Matenge drive up and park his car opposite the open clearing where court was held. Nothing upset Chief Sekoto more than a visit from his brother, whom he had long classified as belonging to the insane part of mankind. He determined to dally over the proceedings for as long as possible in the hope that his brother would become bored and leave. Therefore he turned his full attention on the case at hand.

The case had been brought in from one of the outlying villages, called Bodibeng, and the cause of its rowdiness was that the whole village of Bodibeng had turned up to witness the trial. A certain old woman of the village, named Mma-Baloi, was charged with allegedly practicing witchcraft, and so certain were the villagers of her guilt that they frequently forgot themselves and burst out into loud chatter and had to be brought to order by the president of the court with threats of fines.

Evidence was that Mma-Baloi had always lived a secret and mysterious life apart from the other villagers. She was also in the habit of receiving strangers from far-off places into her home who would not state what dealings they had with Mma-Baloi.

Now, over a certain period, a number of the children of the village had died sudden deaths, and each time a mother stood up to describe these sudden deaths, the crowd roared in fury because the deaths of the children and the evil practices of Mma-Baloi were one and the same thing in their minds. The accused, Mma-Baloi, sat a little apart from the villagers in a quaking, ashen, crumpled heap; and each time the villagers roared, she seemed about to sink into the earth. Noting this, Chief Sekoto's kindly heart was struck with pity.

Further evidence was that about a week ago a strange young woman had turned up in the village of Bodibeng and made straight for the hut of Mma-Baloi, where she had died a sudden death. This had made Mma-Baloi run screaming from her hut, and it was only the intervention of the police that had saved Mma-Baloi from being torn to pieces by the villagers.

Chief Sekoto was silent for some time. The insanity of mankind never ceased to amaze him. At last he turned to the accused and said gently, "Well, mother, what do you have to say in defence of yourself?"

"Sir, I am no witch," said the quavering old voice. "Even though I am called the mother of the witches, I am no witch. Long ago I was taught by the people who live in the bush how to cure ailments with herbs and that is my business."

She pointed a shaking finger at a bag placed near her.

"I would like to see the contents of the bag," Chief Sekoto said with a great show of interest. The bag was brought to him and its contents tipped out on the ground. They were a various assortment of dried leaves, roots, and berries. He examined them leisurely, picking up a few items for closer inspection. This very deliberate gesture was meant to puncture a hole in the confidence of the crowd, who annoyed him. While he fiddled about he was aware of how silent and intent they had become, following his every movement with their eyes. Thus holding the stage, he turned to the old woman and said:

"Proceed with your defence, mother."

"About the deaths of the children of which I am accused, I know nothing, sir," she said. "About the young woman who died in my home last Saturday, I am also innocent. This young woman came to me on recommendation, being grievously ill. We were discussing the ailment when she fell dead at my feet. Never has such a thing occurred before, and this caused me to lose my mind and run out of the house."

"That is quite understandable, mother," Chief Sekoto said sympathetically. "Even I should have been grieved if some stranger was struck with death in my home."

He swept the crowd with a stern glance. "Who issues the certificates of death in Bodibeng?" he asked.

There was a short, bewildered silence. Then a car and a messenger had to be found to fetch the doctor of the Bodibeng hospital. There was a delay of two hours as the doctor was engaged in an operation. Throughout this long wait the court remained in session. At one stage Chief Sekoto recieved an impatient note: "Dear Brother," it said. "Please spare a few moments to discuss an urgent matter."

Chief Sekoto replied: "Is it life or death? I am at the moment faced with the life or death of an old woman. I cannot move."

There was no reply. Chief Sekoto watched his brother's expression out of the corner of his eye. Foremost in the Chief's mind was the necessity to plan an escape route from the glowering thunderstorm. He called the president of the court and whispered, "Ring up George Appleby-Smith and tell him I'm coming to lunch."

It was near noon when the doctor arrived. His evidence was brief and to the point. Yes, it was true, he said. There had been a surprising number of child deaths in the village of Bodibeng, and death in each case had been due to pneumonia; and yes, he said, he had performed a postmortem on the body of a young woman last Saturday afternoon. The young woman had died of a septic womb due to having procured an abortion with a hooked and unsterilized instrument. He would say that the septic condition of the womb had been of three months' duration.

All that was left now was for Chief Sekoto to pass judgment on the case. This he did sternly, drawing himself up to his full height.

"People of Bodibeng," he said. "It seems to me you are all suffering from derangement of the brain."

He paused long enough to allow the villagers to look at each other uneasily.

"Your children die of pneumonia," he thundered, "and to shield yourselves from blame you accuse a poor old woman of having bewitched them into death. Not only that. You falsely accuse her of a most serious crime which carries the death sentence. How long have you planned the death of a poor old woman, deranged people of Bodibeng? How long have you caused her to live in utter misery, suspicion, and fear? I say: Can dogs bark forever? Oh no, people of Bodibeng, today you will make payment for the legs of the old mother who has fled before your barking. I say: The fault is all with you, and because of this I fine each household of Bodibeng one beast. From the money that arises out of the sales of these beasts, each household is to purchase warm clothing for the children so that they may no longer die of pneumonia."

He turned and looked at the old woman, changing his expression to one of kindness.

"As for you, mother," he said. "I cannot allow you to go and live once more among the people of Bodibeng. It is only hatred that the people of Bodibeng feel for you, and this has driven them out of their minds. As hatred never dies, who knows what evil they will not plot against you. I have a large house, and you are welcome to the protection it offers. Besides, I suffer from an ailment for which I am always given penicillin injections at the hospital. Now I am tired of the penicillin injections and perhaps your good herbs may serve to cure me of my troubles."

He stood up, signifying the end of the case. The people of Bodibeng fled in confusion from the courtyard, but the old woman sat for a long time on the ground, silent tears of gratitude dripping down into her lap.

Chief Sekoto walked over briskly to his brother's car, opened a door, and heaved himself inside.

"We must make haste brother," he said. "I have an important appointment to keep."

The first words his brother uttered really surprised Chief Sekoto.

"I wish to be relieved of the administration of Golema Mmidi," said Matenge.

Chief Sekoto furrowed his brow. This was most unexpected. He dreaded what was coming next.

"Have you had another clash with the young man,

Gilbert?" he asked lightly.

Matenge turned his deep doom-ridden eyes on his brother. "He is now harbouring refugees at the farm."

"Oh, is that all, brother?" Chief Sekoto asked, relieved. "I see no harm in that. The world is always full of refugees. How many has Gilbert taken in?"

For answer, Matenge held out the paper with Makhaya's picture on the front page. Chief Sekoto studied the face carefully and felt a sharp stab of jealousy. The man was too attractive, he could steal all the women in the country. Chief Sekoto did not enjoy the thought of a competitor so near his own hunting grounds.

"You mean there is only one refugee, brother?" he asked, anxiously.

Matenge nodded.

"Well, what's the trouble then? Why do you want to resign?"

"I see," Matenge said with heavy sarcasm. "You haven't read the story."

"But I haven't the time, brother. I'm already late for the important appointment."

Matenge swung around furiously on his brother. "Either I go or the refugee goes," he said. "How can people feel safe with a criminal and murderer in their midst? That is what the story says; he is a criminal and murderer who walks around with bombs in his pocket. Why should Gilbert take in such a man unless it is his intention to murder me? There is no other reason why Gilbert should associate with a murderer. He is doing nothing at the farm."

Chief Sekoto edged towards the door. "Brother," he said. "Such criminology is outside my jurisdiction. You must report this matter to the police. You must report this to George Appleby-Smith as he patrols your area. In the meantime, please avail yourself of my hospitality and have lunch at the house. Tell the wife I am called away by an important appointment."

Chief Sekoto swung his short dumpy legs out of the car, closed the door and, without looking back, waddled over briskly to a small white sports car. He was literally suffocating. Inside the fat, overstuffed body was a spirit that fiercely resented intense, demanding, vicious people. It was as though they had the power to trap him inside a dark airless tunnel when all he wanted was the casualness of the free air and the silly chatter of a pretty, painted-up woman.

The small white car roared into life. Chief Sekoto pressed the accelerator down to the floor and then, at a speed of over a hundred miles an hour, streaked out of the village like a continuous blur of white light. Within barely fifteen minutes he had covered twenty-eight miles and approached the railroad crossing where Makhaya had been dropped off by the truck driver on his first day in Botswana. The chief slowed down, drove past the railway station and into a yard which contained a small white-washed house. It was the home of his friend, Inspector George Appleby-Smith, the green-eyed police officer who had interviewed Makhaya and granted him political asylum.

George Appleby-Smith was twenty years younger than Chief Sekoto, and yet a strong bond of friendship existed between the two men. They had known each other for five years and often went hunting for game in the bush together. Game-hunting was George's chief passion, but he was abnormally afraid of snakes, so Chief Sekoto's gun was always reserved for shooting at snakes. Jokes were a favourite topic of conversation on these excursions.

For example, George would inquire, "Tell me, Chief, what's the difference between a barber and a sculptor?"

A long interval of silence would ensue during which

Chief Sekoto furrowed his brows vigorously. At last he'd say, "I must say I don't really know, George."

"Well, it's like this, Chief. The sculptor makes faces and busts and the barber curls up and dyes."

The collection of these droll jokes was George's leisure-time hobby. He had a way of holding all the laughter of the world in his eyes, yet he rarely smiled and rarely twitched a muscle on his face. He liked his work and was very dedicated. Yet he summed up law and order and all pompous phrases in one expressive word: Bullshit. What he liked in all the bullshit was people. They were like a complicated crossword puzzle to him. They exercised his agile, inventive mind which had a peculiar ability to streamline the complex into a single and clear detail. Nothing alarmed a prisoner more than to be told by George that he was not speaking the truth, and it was the blunt and authoritative manner in which he said this that always unnerved them.

Chief Sekoto never summed up for himself why it was George's company so delighted him, but both were casual, freedom-loving men, and they only parted company on their ideas on women and food. George, being a bachelor, ate terrible food. It was always soup with a little bit of cheese on the plate, while Chief Sekoto usually ate roast leg of mutton for dinner. But somehow George managed to serve roast leg of mutton when Chief Sekoto came to dine.

George was already seated at table when Chief Sekoto walked into the dining-room and said:

"I'm a little upset today, George. Have you got any beer to calm my nerves?"

George stood up, went to the kitchen and returned with a glass and a small bottle of beer. Chief Sekoto looked anxiously at his friend. When George was silent and kept his face expressionless, it was a sure sign that he had something on his mind.

"Don't tell me I've run away from troubles, only to find you have troubles too, George," he said in despair.

George looked down at his plate to hide the laughter in his eyes. "I saw your brother heading past this way, Chief," he said, quietly. "Did he by any chance visit you?"

Chief Sekoto was silent for some time. "I don't really understand my brother," he said, glumly. "I gave him a position that was meant to protect him from the wrath of his enemies. At the time he was plotting my death many people said: 'You should have this brother of yours killed.' I said: 'No, leave the man to his Maker.' And what payment have I received for this generosity? Nothing but trouble. Golema Mmidi is now famous for trouble, and if that is not enough, my brother comes to me today and tells me that Gilbert is plotting his death and has especially employed a dangerous refugee to help him."

George stared reflectively at the wall, and after some time said softly, "Chief, would you mind if I put your brother in jail?"

Chief Sekoto leaned forward, interested. "For how long?" he asked.

"I don't know," George replied. "It's just a feeling. Some people are on tenterhooks about his association with Joas Tsepe. Tsepe is under the illusion that he will be able to establish a secret military camp in the bush. He has no idea that his every movement is known. The day he smuggles those guns over the border, he's in for the high jump. If you like, we can delay matters until he brings your brother into the deal and we rope him in as well."

Chief Sekoto nodded his head vigorously. "I've no objection to my brother going to jail, George," he said. "Only it must be for a long time. But what about the refugee? My brother wants him removed."

"It's not what he wants," George said, calmly. "But what I want. What I want is for Gilbert to carry on with his work because everyone else is bullshitting around."

Chief Sekoto laughed heartily. "I made a promise to Gilbert that I would come and work on his farm if it succeeds," he said. "Now I see that with your help, my friend, I shall be spending my old age in hard labour. But you must promise me something. You must spy on the refugee and tell me if he is eating up all the women."

George looked affectionately at the old man, marvelling at his ability to take everything in life so lightly. Some other man might be ranting and raving by now, after all that had happened. The chief's eldest son, with whom he had quarrelled, had brought the anti-chief policy into government. It wasn't a ruthless policy. In fact, there was an over-all recognition of the hold custom and tradition had on the lives of the people, and in deference to this, all chiefs' salaries had been increased. A chief was still a father figure but somehow thrust to one side, the accent being on nation rather than tribe. Nonentities had been raised up from the dust by the people's vote, and it was they who now reigned supreme on the local government councils. If George Appleby-Smith felt a pang of regret at the death of the old order, it was because life had been simpler with the decisions and power in the hands of one man. If it was complex now it was because chiefs had had a long reign and deeply resented relegation to the status of rubber stamp. Whereas in former times a chief was the upholder of law and order, in these days he consorted with strange fellows who were hell-bent on blowing everything up, and who glibly promised to restore to him his lost political influence. Few chiefs appreciated the salary increase. Many voiced complaints about the younger generation, who no longer bowed the knee but merely politely raised their hats. The chiefs were unable to see that people could not go on being children forever and their humble servants. True enough, the change itself was not dramatic. Even Chief Sekoto still kept his unpaid slaves. But George, with one foot in the past and his youthfulness in the present, was very emotionally involved in upholding the aims of the new, conservative government which wanted everything to happen bit by bit. He was prepared to deal deathblows to any forces that planned its premature overthrow.

"I can promise you I'll spy on the refugee, Chief," he said, with mock grimness. "Even though it will delay my own promotion by five years. 'So George has now gone soft on refugees?' they'll say. 'We knew we couldn't trust the bugger.'"

He looked at his watch and regretfully parted company with his amiable friend. The lunch-hour break for him was over. Chief Sekoto remained, eating and drinking at a leisurely pace. The cunning old man was waiting for his brother to pass and return to his own village, and only then would he get into his car and streak back home.

A short while later he heard the approach of a car. He stood up and peered out of a window and saw his brother draw up outside the police station, get out of the car and walk to the office of George Appleby-Smith. After five minutes, his brother emerged and without looking around walked straight to his car, climbed in, and drove in the direction of Golema Mmidi. Not believing his good luck, Chief Sekoto waited until the cream Chevrolet had disappeared in the dust, and breathing a sigh of relief, he walked out to his own car. But just then he saw George Appleby-Smith walk out of his office towards a grey police Land-Rover. The chief watched George drive off after his brother in the direction of Golema Mmidi. Chief Sekoto closed his eyes. What would happen now? Since he could not bear to think about it, he heaved himself into the car and drove back home at an ungodly speed.

George too was a fast driver. He soon passed Matenge and within twenty minutes arrived in Golema Mmidi and drove up to the farm gates. No one was in sight. Out on the farm fields, the five specially hired and government-trained tractor drivers were doing the winter ploughing. He parked the Land-Rover outside the farm gate, lifted the wire latch, and walked in the direction of a small brick building which was the farm office. There he found Gilbert and Makhaya, standing at a table, absorbed in the study of a map. The map was a plan of the farm's fields, and Gilbert was filling in the crops he intended planting during the coming season.

The two men looked up at his entry. George Appleby-Smith was apologetic. He profoundly respected Gilbert.

"I won't take up much time," he said. "Please fill in this form, Mr. Maseko. It's an application for residence. I have to take it back with me."

Makhaya took the form but he was a little surprised. It had not occurred to him to apply for residence in Botswana. George walked up to the table and studied the map. To one plot Gilbert had allocated Turkish tobacco.

"Don't tell me you're going to grow tobacco in this desert," he said, amazed.

"Why not?" Gilbert said. "Golema Mmidi has the exact amount of rainfall of a certain area in southern Africa where Turkish tobacco is grown very successfully. It's a very good cash crop too, and if everyone in Golema Mmidi grows a bit and we market it co-operatively—why, we'll all be rich in no time. The only problem we're faced with is the flatness of the land. It needs a slight slope and well-drained soil. We'll either have to create this artificially or lay down pipes."

George Appleby-Smith was very impressed, and after this made a great show of minding his own business by staring at a wall. Gilbert glanced at him slyly, smiled to himself and continued his work.

Makhaya completed the form and handed it to the police officer, who looked at him in an odd quizzical way.

"Step outside with me for a moment, Mr. Maseko," he said.

They walked for a moment in silence towards the gate, then George stopped abruptly.

"Chief Matenge, who administers this village, wants you removed from it on the grounds that you're a refugee," he said. "What he wants has never really mattered to me. We don't see eye to eye. But this time he has a point. The government doesn't encourage refugees. It would like you all to push off somewhere."

Makhaya kept silent, not knowing what to say.

"In fact," George Appleby-Smith continued. "Things are so bad that if anyone sticks his neck out for a refugee, he's not likely to get promoted for five years."

"You mean you'll stick your neck out for me?" Makhaya asked, amused.

"That's what I'm saying, but only on the guarantee that you don't let me down and mess around in the politics of southern Africa."

"You don't have to bother," Makhaya said, sharply annoyed. "I'm not begging anyone in this country to shove me around."

The green eyes blazed with anger. "Don't give me that bullshit," George shot out. "And if you've got any bullshitting chip on your shoulder, keep it to yourself."

They stared at each other in this brief flare of anger. Makhaya was the first to regain his humour.

"Tie a man's hands behind his back and then ask him if he's going to chop down a tree," he said, smiling. "I wish the whole of southern Africa would go to hell. Only I don't know what to do about getting it there."

"Smart guy," George drawled, also smiling. "It's not your philosophy of life I'm after, but a straight, practical 'yes' or 'no'. Are you going to leave politics alone?"

Makhaya looked at him with a pained expression. "No, I won't," he said. "I may have run myself into a dead end. I may be sick of everything, but the day I fix myself up, I'll do whatever I think is the right thing to do."

George Appleby-Smith looked at him for some time. "I'll still stick my neck out for you," he said, quietly.

He half-turned to go, then remembered something. "Report your presence in this village to Chief Matenge tomorrow morning at eight. He's responsible for the comings and goings of people and has to know, for the record, whether you intend staying here."

He walked to his Land-Rover, climbed in, and drove off. Makhaya remained where he was some minutes longer. If there was anything he liked on earth, it was human generosity. It made life seem whole and sane to him. It kept the world from shattering into tiny fragments. Only a few, quietly spoken words: "I'll still stick my neck out for you."

As he entered the office, Gilbert looked up and smiled. "What did that funny cop have to say?" he asked.

"Nothing much," Makhaya said. "Except that I should report my presence in the village to Chief Matenge tomorrow morning."

Chapter 5

Chief Matenge really believed he was "royalty". So deeply ingrained was this belief in him that he had acquired a number of personal possessions to bolster the image. One was a high-backed kingly chair and the other was a deep purple, tasselled and expensive dressing gown. In this royal purple gown, he paced up and down the porch of his mansion every morning, lost in a Napoleon-like reverie. Of late, this pacing had been often done to the accompaniment of loud chatter from Joas Tsepe. Loud is perhaps an understatement of Joas's speech. He was a platform speaker who never got down from the platform. He was hoarse-voiced. He was always in a sweat. He gesticulated. He had attended so many conferences that his ordinary speech was forever an underlined address: "Mr. Chairman, and fellow delegates . . ."

Usually, Matenge paid little attention. Joas came from a certain tribe of the Kalahari Desert who were still regarded as slaves. The chief also despised the literature of Joas's political party. In this respect he reflected the attitude of his country. The tide of African nationalism had swept down the continent and then faltered at the northern borders of Botswana. During the pre-election campaign, the politicians had had to chase after the people who kept on moving back and forth to their cattle posts and lands, seemingly unaware that destiny was about to catch up with them. But they couldn't get away from the blaring microphones, and after a time they paused awhile, to listen. One crowd of politicians shouted that the people should take up arms, and embark upon the "Unbroken Line" with "freedom" as their grand aim. You have nothing to lose but your chains, they were told. People listened with mounting anxiety. They could well enough see that they were important to these men.

But what did it all mean? What was this "Unbroken Line" and where were the chains? The politicians could not perceive that the conference table terms meant little to a people who never read a newspaper and who were completely out of touch with the latest trends, but they pushed ahead all the same, glibly spouting the meaningless phrases. They invaded people's homes on hut-to-hut campaigns, blindly gesticulating and shouting that they were "in the grip of the force and direction of the law of change," as they were wont to call this new phenomenon, African nationalism.

The other political party—the sons and relatives of chiefs—was more cunning. It kept its distance. It played catchy little folk songs everyone knew. It talked about cattle and crops and all the familiar Botswana problems. People were soothed, perhaps even a little disappointed. The latter crowd was too well known; all their faults and failings and private evils were openly discussed in the villages.

Then the pamphlets started circulating, each party stating its views. The sons of chiefs collected the data from the experts and issued neat little manifestos outlining the problems of the country—water, agriculture, cattle development. The sons of slaves attacked the "imperialists and neo-colonialists" who were still skillfully manipulating the affairs of an oppressed people. But they put over their ideas very badly, with many spelling errors:

"You will get a pseudo-independence if you do not vote for us," the pamphlets stated. "Do not stamble. We are people in the clear who know the line. We will eliminate ignorant disease."

It was one of the most pathetic of elections. The sons of chiefs, who had had all the advantages of education, pounced on the spelling errors of the sons of slaves, who had little or no education.

"Can such men run a country?" they asked, gleefully.

Thus, driven with their backs to the wall, the sons of slaves resorted to low-down mud-slinging. The chiefs all had syphilis, they said. For such defamatory statements, many served jail sentences. Others, like Joas, were imprisoned for getting voters to sign papers on the pretext that his party and the party of chiefs were one and the same thing. For all this, the sons of slaves found themselves more despised than they had ever been before.

Matenge, being educated, soon cast aside the literature of Pan-Africanism. But Joas as a person made sense to him. His own crooked mind and Joas's crooked mind tallied. Besides, Joas had a remarkable amount of inside information on Matenge's arch enemy, Gilbert.

"I'll tell you what the Imperialists are up to now, Chief," he said one day. "First they sent the missionaries. Now they send volunteers like Gilbert. What is a volunteer? Volunteer, my eye. I have top-secret information about these training camps in England. Gilbert has been sent here to pave the way for the second scramble for Africa."

This particular morning, Joas was hopping mad. He stood in one corner of the porch, gesticulating, fuming, his eyes almost darting out of his head in self-righteous indignation. On the previous day he had approached a registrar of co-operatives in an attempt to get his cattle co-operatively registered.

"And do you know what Smedley said to me, Chief? He said, 'I'm afraid I can't register your co-operative, Mr. Tsepe.' I said, 'And why not?' And he said, 'I'm not going to allow co-operatives to be used for political propaganda.' So I said, 'But everyone is a politician these days, Mr. Smedley. Why discriminate against me? A certain other person I know got his co-operative registered in one day. Aren't you practising racialism, Mr. Smedley? This matter won't rest between you and me. I am going to report . . .'"

Matenge held up his hand with a sudden, imperious gesture. In his pacing he had noticed the approach of Makhaya, accompanied by the old man, Dinorego. Matenge stared intently at Makhaya and made several errors in his summing up. The flinching, averted face and slightly hunched-forward shoulders, he interpreted as the sign of a weak and cowardly character. And the very marked air of calmness in the long strides, he associated with the type of man who would never put up a battle.

Matenge slowly descended the steps. The descent was regal, kingly, spectacular. Makhaya jerked up his head in surprise. The sham of it all appealed to his sense of humour, but one look at the face of Matenge instantly aroused his sympathy. It was the face of a tortured man, slowly being devoured by the intensity of his inner life, and the tormented hell of that inner life had scarred deep ridges across his brow and down his cheeks, and the icy peaks of loneliness on which the man lived had only experienced the storms and winters of life, never the warm dissolving sun of love. Being himself a lonely man, Makhaya instinctively sensed this. But they differed. Makhaya's was a self-protective loneliness, and he had the sun inside him all the time.

Dinorego politely bowed his head and greeted Matenge. His greeting was dismissed with a slight gesture of the head, which contained in it an inheritance of centuries of contempt for the ordinary man. Matenge never once took his eyes off Makhaya, as though by this concentrated stare he intended to pulverize Makhaya into nonexistence.

"Who are you?" he asked.

"Makhaya Maseko."

Matenge bent his head slightly and a mocking smile played around his mouth. "I hear you have begun to work with Gilbert at the farm," he said.

"It worries me," he said. "Gilbert just makes arrangements with people but the authorities do not approve of his actions, nor the people he chooses to associate with. Having a refugee at the farm is going to give it a bad name, including the whole area in which it is placed."

"What's wrong with a refugee?" Makhaya asked.

"Oh, we hear things about them," he said. "They get up at night and batter people to death."

He glanced briefly at Dinorego, then continued, "I'll tell you something about Gilbert. He knows nothing about Botswana agriculture. He ought to be in England where he received his training in agriculture. The only man who knows how to do things here is a Batswana man. Most of the trouble here is caused by people from outside and we don't want you. We want you to get out. When are you going?"

Makhaya looked at the man in amazement and disbelief, almost overwhelmed by the viciousness in his voice.

"But I'm not going away," Makhaya said, as calmly as he could, though a sudden rush of anger made his voice quiver.

"If you don't go away I'll make things difficult for you here," he said.

"What else can I say, except go ahead?" Makhaya said.

Matenge smiled. "You know what a South African swine is?" he said. "He is a man like you. He always needs to run after his master, the white man."

Matenge turned and ascended the steps, unaware that a murderously angry man stood staring up at him. There was a wild element in Makhaya. He had seen and faced death too often to be afraid of it, and taking another man's life meant little to him. Several times Dinorego said, "Let's go, my son." But Makhaya just looked at the old man with a pained, dazed expression and his eyes glistened with tears. Dinorego misinterpreted this, and tears also rushed into his eyes.

Joas Tsepe ran lightly down the steps. "I'd like a word with you, Maseko," he said.

Makhaya laughed harshly, sarcastically. "I don't know who you are," he said. "But Maseko is my father's name and I haven't given you permission to use it."

He turned abruptly and walked away. Dinorego shuffled anxiously beside him. He kept glancing at Makhaya's face but could not understand his mood. It was tight and withdrawn.

"I am struck with pity for what has happened, my son," he said. "But you must keep calm. Some people say the chief has high blood pressure and will surely die of this ailment one day."

Makhaya looked at the old man with a queer expression. "The chief is not going to die of high blood pressure," he said. "I am going to kill him."

And he said this with all the calm assurance of a fortune-teller making a prediction. Dinorego went ashen with shock.

"No," he said sharply. "You must never, never do that, my son."

"But he is concentrating on killing someone," Makhaya said.

"And he is doing this, not with guns or blows, but through the cruelty and cunning of his mind."

Dinorego absorbed this rapidly. It had a strange ring of truth. The series of crises and upheavals in Golema Mmidi fully justified Makhaya's theory.

"Can't you concentrate too, son," the old man said quickly. "Can't you concentrate and be as clever as the next man?"

This quaint reply and the anxiety of the old man completely dashed away Makhaya's anger. He laughed but he also felt a twinge of remorse. Makhaya felt that anger had made him utter unduly harsh words to that other grinning, uncomfortable fellow who had run down the steps. Perhaps he was just another of those two-penny-ha'penny politicians who sprang up everywhere like mushrooms in Africa these days.

"Who is the other man?" he asked.

"His name is Joas Tsepe," Dinorego said. "He and the chief are acting like spies against the new government."

"Is the new government popular?"

"Oh yes," said Dinorego. "It is very popular. People can vote for it for twenty years. Men like Joas do not speak the language of the people. Who can understand cheating and murder when such things are not the custom here? Some say the new government cannot improve people's lives because the leaders come from the chiefs. But we can wait and see, and if they are no good, one day we will chuck them out."

They turned out of the circular clearing in the central part of the village and took the road that led back to the farm.

"What is the time, son?" Dinorego asked. "I want to introduce you to my friend Mma-Millipede. She is anxious to meet you and cannot wait any longer."

Makhaya looked at his watch. It was eight fifteen. And there was a twenty-minute walk back to the farm. The old man shook his head.

"I cannot trust my friend Mma-Millipede," he said. "She will delay us."

But Makhaya waved this aside. On the way to Chief Matenge, the old man had told him a very moving story about Mma-Millipede and the great tragedy in her life.

Mma-Millipede, he had said, had grown up side by side with him in a village in the northern part of Botswana. The mother of Mma-Millipede and his mother were such great friends that they privately arranged a marriage for their two children at some future date.

It so happened that while growing up Mma-Millipede became very interested in the Christian religion. On the surface this was not unusual. Women lived idly in the villages during the dry season while the men were busy the year round with the cattle. To fill in the dull round of the day, many women drifted to the church, where they were also able to obtain a bit of mission education. But in spite of the advantage they had over men educationally, few of the women developed a new personality. They remained their same old tribal selves, docile and inferior. Perhaps Mma-Millipede was one of those rare individuals with a distinct personality at birth. In any event, she was able to grasp the religion of the missionaries and use its message to adorn and enrich her own originality of thought and expand the natural kindness of her heart.

The family of Mma-Millipede was one of the poorest in the village. But the recognition Mma-Millipede had gained for her religious views soon brought her to the attention of the chiefs, in particular one named Ramogodi, a drunkard and dissipated boaster and the son of the reigning chief. It was Ramogodi's pride that he was sexually attractive to women. This was true. There were few women in the village who had not been his bedmate at some time or other. But whenever he waylaid Mma-Millipede, she just stared at him, seriously. Thus, Mma-Millipede unconsciously challenged the pride of a vain man, and he became determined to have her as his wife.

His haughty mother approached Mma-Millipede's family. They refused to offer their daughter in marriage to a chief's son, fearing that she would be treated as a slave in the household. The haughty woman interpreted this refusal as an insult to the royal house and proceeded with plans to force the marriage.

She found out about the proposed marriage of Mma-Millipede to Dinorego and forced Dinorego's parents to arrange another bride for him with all speed. Thus, terrorized into submission, the family of Mma-Millipede had no choice but to allow their daughter to marry Ramogodi. There was only one child from the marriage, because Mma-Millipede and her religious ways soon bored Ramogodi. He was often away from home, making hay with his former sweethearts. Still, Mma-Millipede continued to live in his house as his wife and bring up their son.

After many years came trouble. The youngest brother of Ramogodi acquired a very beautiful wife, and Ramogodi took it into his head that he also desired the same woman. Things came to such a pass that Ramogodi's brother committed suicide by hanging himself. He left a note saying: "I cannot stand the way my brother is carrying on with my wife."

This made Ramogodi the most hated man in the village, but in spite of that, he divorced Mma-Millipede and within three months married his brother's wife. The son of Mma-Millipede had to be exiled to a far-off village because he could not be restrained from the urge to kill his father. The shock of it all almost deranged the mind of Mma-Millipede, and in an effort to help her forget the past, Dinorego and his wife persuaded her to come and live with them in Golema Mmidi, where they had settled. A few years later Dinorego's wife died of heart trouble, but the long and close friendship between Dinorego and Mma-Millipede continued. Mma-Millipede had become a trader of all kinds, and she also purchased the skins of wild animals, which Dinorego made into mats and blankets.

As Dinorego and Makhaya approached the home of Mma-Millipede, which was not very far from the home of Dinorego, they turned off onto a small footpath that wound and curved its way into the bush. The sudden clearing revealed the identical pattern of mud huts perched on the edge of the land. The yard was crowded with children. There were a lot of goats, and Makhaya got the impression of goats and children rolling in the dust.

"The children belong to the families of Golema Mmidi," Dinorego said, smiling. "They are supposed to be out in the bush grazing the goats, but here they are all playing at the home of Mma-Millipede. I told her she will one day become bankrupt through having to feed all these children and goats, but she pays no attention."

An old woman walked slowly across the yard in a forward-bending manner as though her back troubled her. She wore a very long dress and had a scarf tied round her head. The children set up a clamour when they saw Dinorego, and she swerved round in her walk.

"Batho!" she said, addressing Dinorego. "But I say, you are about early today, my friend."

"I have brought my son about whom we spoke the whole week," he replied.

"Batho!" she said, again.

She turned and looked at Makhaya, closely. There was something so lovely in the expression of habitual good humour and kindness in her face that it evoked a spontaneous smile in him. Once he got to know her well, he was to find that she often prefaced sentences with the word "Batho," which means "Oh, People" and may be used to express either sympathy, joy, or surprise.

Whatever conclusions the old woman had come to through her inspection of Makhaya's face, she determined to keep to herself and discuss them with the old man once Makhaya had left. To indicate this, she glanced meaningfully at Dinorego from under her eyes.

In reply Dinorego said, "My son cannot stay long. He is just on his way to work."

"Indeed! I am ashamed of you, my friend. What about the tea? There is always time for tea. Besides, I must gather some eggs to send to Gilbert. I was just about to feed the fowls."

She pointed to a basket in her hand which was full of corn seed. This made Makhaya look towards the chicken house and recall the vivid words of the old man on their first day of meeting: "If you have fifty-two fowls, you must build a coop fifteen feet by twenty-five feet . . ." And indeed, the chicken house stretched the entire length of the yard. Three of its walls were built up of a mixture of smoothed mud and bricks, while the front part was enclosed with chicken wire and had a small gate. Poles were spaced at neat intervals round the walls, over which was suspended a thatched roof. There were troughs for food and water and boxes for broody hens. Fat sleek fowls pecked in the dust.

A child emerged from one of the huts with a tea tray, and once they had seated themselves, Mma-Millipede wanted to know all sorts of little things about Makhaya. Do you eat well, my son? she asked. Do you often get ill? If you get ill, please inform me so that I may accompany you to hospital as you are now far away from your home and relatives. About all these small things she chattered in her kindly motherly way, and they seemed like mountains of affection to the lonely Makhaya. He noted how the old man nodded his head contentedly in this sun of kindness and how the goats kept frisking their short tails and raising their forelegs high in the air, pretending to crack each other's skulls in mock battles, while the children tumbled in the dust. He was a little repelled at first by the generosity of the strange old woman. It was too extreme. It meant that if you loved people you had to allow a complete invasion by them of your life, and he wasn't built to face invasions of any kind. And yet, this isolation he so treasured had often been painful, because he too felt this eternal human need to share the best and worst of life with another. Thus he looked at the old woman questioningly. He wanted a few simple answers on how to live well and sanely. He wanted to undo the complexity of hatred and humiliation that had dominated his life for so long. Perhaps, he thought, her life might provide him with a few clues.

Makhaya would have been amused at the chatter of the old people once he had left.

"I say, my friend," Mma-Millipede burst out excitedly. "The young man is too handsome. Can you imagine all the trouble if he is not of good character? I am even afraid to think of it."

She was thinking of all the men who were away at the cattle posts and the mines and how Golema Mmidi was just a village of women for the greater part of the year.

"I was thinking that the young man would make a good husband for my daughter," Dinorego said. "What do you think, my friend?"

Mma-Millipede looked at her friend for some time.

She had a lot of reservations about Maria. Even her shrewd eye had not succeeded in penetrating the barrier of aloofness and hostility that were a natural part of the young girl's personality. But she had long suspected that there was more than met the eye in the friendship between Maria and Gilbert. It had been of such a long duration that almost everyone had come to take it for granted, in particular her good friend. The only thing that prevented Mma-Millipede from voicing her suspicions to her friend was the fact that, to her, Gilbert was a foreign man, and foreign men were a fearful unpredictable quantity in an otherwise predictable world.

"I shall have a talk with the child, my friend," she said at last. "I shall try to find out for you what is on her mind."

Back at the mansion, Matenge was reviewing the short interview he had had with Makhaya. He was reviewing it intensely, in a one-track way.

"So the refugee says he's not leaving," and he said this over and over, staring sightlessly at the grinning Joas Tsepe. Tsepe, too, was still smarting under the rough snub given him by Makhaya. Joas was not the kind of man who could stop and examine himself. He could not see how unpleasant his too familiar manner was to other people, and he would never know that the inferiority complex, which was the driving force of his life, was also a dangerous little bully.

"I can sum up a man like that from a mile, Chief," he said. "He's a traitor to the African cause."

Eventually, Matenge's one-track sentence drove him to his car and to the office of Inspector George Appleby-Smith.

"The refugee says he's not going," he said, looking down into the expressionless face of the police officer. "I have made an ultimatum. I want him removed because he is a dangerous criminal who is using the farm as his hideaway. No one is safe in my village. I don't see how the authorities can allow him to remain there."

"I quite get your point, Chief Matenge," the officer said. "The only thing is that the matter is no longer in my hands. It is now the responsibility of the chief immigration officer, Major Ross. He has promised me he will make a decision concerning Mr. Maseko in one week's time."

After Matenge had walked out, George Appleby-Smith remained staring at the wall ahead of him for a long time. He had not so very long ago been on the phone with Major Ross, had "stuck his neck out", as he said he would, and been assured that Makhaya would be granted a resident permit in one week. His assistant-in-command of the station entered and had to click his heels several times before he gained the attention of his superior. George Appleby-Smith looked at him with laughter-filled eyes.

"Sergeant Molefe," he said. "Tell me why I hate people?"

The sergeant remained stiffly at attention. He was used to the oddities of George Appleby-Smith. "I think you only hate people when you have a headache, sir," he said.

Once the week was up, Matenge took it upon himself to drive the three hundred miles down to immigration headquarters, perhaps hoping to influence the decision concerning Makhaya's removal. He knew everything was on his side. Political refugees were never allowed permanent residence in Botswana, and it did not take too many complaints to engineer their removal.

But the major hummed and hawed a bit and made a show of looking through a file, then dropped a bombshell.

"Makhaya Maseko," he said. "Ah . . . let me see.

Here it is. We found out that he qualified for residence and granted him a resident permit yesterday. It is already on its way to him."

That inner howling devil once more retreated. Matenge walked out crumpled, and each time he faced a defeat his eyes would get a peculiar hollow look in them and he would quicken his pace in walking. Particularly someone in a superior position to him could make him crumple this way. On this occasion, the shock was accompanied by fear. He felt his position threatened, and he felt that the threat to his position was his association with Joas Tsepe. He felt that the granting of the resident permit to a refugee was to spite him for his association with Joas. He determined to rid himself of the company of Joas Tsepe. Fortunately for Joas Tsepe, his political party just at this time sent him away for six months on an important "mission".

In the meanwhile, shortly after his failure to banish Makhaya, Matenge was struck down with a severe attack of high blood pressure. He was in hospital for one month, and during this one month a number of rapid changes took place in Golema Mmidi and at the farm.

Chapter 6

One might go so far as to say that it is strong, dominating personalities who play a decisive role when things are changing. Somehow they always manage to speak with the voice of authority, and their innate strength of character drives them to take the lead in almost any situation. Allied to all this is their boundless optimism and faith in their fellow men. One such personality in the village of Golema Mmidi was Dinorego, and it was his support of and belief in Gilbert that swayed the villagers over to a support of the cattle co-operative. Another such personality was Paulina Sebeso, who was to bring the women of the village to the farm and help open up the way for new agricultural developments in Golema Mmidi.

Paulina Sebeso was quite a newcomer to the village, having lived there for not more than a year and a half by the time Makhaya arrived. She came from the northern part of Botswana, which fact immediately ensured her the friendship of Dinorego and Mma-Millipede. Northerners really pride themselves on being inexplicable to the rest of the country. They speak Tswana at a faster, almost unintelligible pace and have added so much variety to the Tswana language as to seem to an outsider to be speaking a completely foreign tongue. Thus, when northerners greet each other they say: Good-day, branch-of-my-tree; while everyone else simply says: Good-day, friend.

The implication in the greeting, branch-of-my-tree, was a rather true one for northerners. At one time they had been the most closely knit of all the tribal groupings, each one claiming at least a distant relationship to even the most insignificant member of the clan. But, once the family structure began breaking down under the migratory labour system, it was they who most readily practised intermarriage with foreigners.

Unfortunately for Paulina Sebeso, she married, at the age of eighteen, a foreign man from Rhodesia whose tribal tradition it was to commit suicide when his honour was at stake. It wasn't a remarkable marriage and her husband wasn't a remarkable man, being rather of a mild, passive, stay-at-home temperament. He worked as a bookkeeper for a certain large company, for which he received a wage of thirty pounds a month. By careful saving he managed to build a two-room brick house for his family, and also every year added a heifer or two to their stock of cattle. He had worked for the company for sixteen years when a new manager was appointed. Before long the new manager claimed that two thousand pounds had been embezzled. He also produced evidence that a number of receipt books were missing. The only people who handled both the money and the books were Paulina's husband and the manager. There was a doubt. On the one hand, the company believed the claim of Paulina's husband that he was innocent of the crime. He had worked for them for a long time, was known to be of sober habits and the sum stolen was too large an amount to have been stolen by an African man. Petty pilferings had occurred here and there but never vast sums. On the other hand, the receipt books had been removed in such a skilful manner as to suggest that the embezzling had taken place over a number of years.

In the end the company charged both Paulina's husband and the new manager with the theft. On the day he was notified of this, Paulina's husband awoke in the night and hung himself from a tree in the yard.

He left a note, once again claiming innocence. The company, being anxious to regain its money, dropped the court case and immediately seized the property of the dead man, claiming that the suicide was in fact an admission of guilt. Thus, being dispossessed of a home almost overnight, Paulina moved, with a son aged ten and a daughter aged eight, to the village of Golema Mmidi. The son, named Isaac, lived at a cattle post twenty-five miles away, herding his mother's cattle while Paulina and the small girl remained in the village to grow crops. The eight-year-old girl, named Lorato, was thus able for most of the year to attend the village primary school, while the boy, Isaac, was tied to the cattle post and received no education at all.

Perhaps Paulina was not a very beautiful woman. She was tall, thin and angular, with a thin, angular face. She was also flat-chested and like all flat-chested women, this was a sore point with her. It was hard to find a suitable stuffed-up breast bodice in a country like Botswana, especially if you have to live in the bush, so she was in the habit of stuffing hers with carefully crumpled bits of paper. But she had lovely big black eyes that stared at everything in a bold way, and her long straight black legs were the most beautiful legs in the village. She had a decisive way of walking as though she always knew where she was going and what she wanted. She was fond of gaudy-hued skirts with strong colours like orange and yellow and red, and the bigger and brighter the splashes of colour, the more she liked them.

Since she was not by temperament given to brooding on the past, she soon recovered from the tragedy in her life and set out to build up a new life in Golema Mmidi. Part of her plans also included a man, as she was a passionate and impetuous woman with a warm heart. It never really mattered what kind of man he was or the magnitude of his faults and failings. It was just enough that her feelings be aroused and everything would be swallowed up in a blinding sun of devotion and loyalty. Of course, if she were to find a man who accidentally managed to gain the respect of the whole world at the same time, then this loved one could magically become ten thousand blazing suns.

She had her land and home not far from the farm gates. There, directly in the path of the setting sun, Makhaya was in the habit of coming to watch the sunset. Just as at dawn, the sun crept along the ground in gold shafts; so at sundown it retreated quietly as though it were folding into itself the long brilliant fingers of light. As he watched it all in fascination, the pitch black shadows of night seemed to sweep across the land like an engulfing wave. One minute the sun was there, and the next minute it had dropped down behind the flat horizon, plunging everything into darkness. On intensely cold nights, it threw up a translucent yellow afterglow, full of sparkling crystals, but otherwise it puffed itself out into a thin strip of red light on the horizon. As his eyes became more and more accustomed to the peculiar beauty of Botswana sunsets, he also noticed that the dull green thornbush and the dull brown earth were transformed into autumn shades of warm brown, red, and yellow hues by the setting sun.

One evening, Makhaya walked right into a great drama. The thornbush was seeding and it did this in a vigorous way. One spray of seed struck him on the cheek, and on a closer inspection, he noticed that all the branches were profusely covered with beanlike pods. These pods twined tightly inward until they were coiled springs. Once the pod burst, the spring ejected the seeds high into the air. He stretched out his hand, broke off a pod and pressed it open. A few minute kidney-bean-shaped seeds slithered on to his palm. He stared at them in amazement. Could this rough, tough little thornbush be a relative of the garden bean? He decided to take the seeds back to the farm and question Gilbert.

Paulina, meanwhile, had watched these comings and goings at sundown with avid curiosity and at last, being unable to contain it, had sent the little girl to Makhaya with a message. This particular evening Makhaya stood just a stone's throw away from her yard, and being absorbed as he was in the popping, spraying drama around him, he did not at first notice the child standing near him. And even when he did, he looked down rather absentmindedly into a pair of small beady black eyes.

"Sir," the child said. "My mother says she sends you her greetings."

"Who is your mother?" he asked.

The child pointed in the direction of the huts. Makhaya glanced up briefly, was struck in the eye by a vivid sunset skirt of bright orange and yellow flowers and momentarily captivated by a pair of large bold black eyes. He looked down at the child and sent back a cruel message.

"Go and tell your mother I don't know her," he said.

He turned and, without looking either left or right, walked back to the farm. Paulina, on receiving his message, flamed with confusion and humiliation. So distressed was she that she rushed over to her friend Mma-Millipede.

"Mama," she said. "I've made a terrible blunder."

And, half-hiding her face in her hands, she explained her blunder.

"You've done nothing wrong, my child," Mma-Millipede said, calmly. "It's just that Makhaya is a foreign man and not accustomed to our ways. The women of his country might have an entirely different approach when they wish to arouse the interest of a man."

Paulina sat in thoughtful silence for a while. As far as she was concerned, there was only one woman equal to her in the whole village.

"Perhaps he is attracted to Maria," she said, and it nearly killed her to utter these words.

Mma-Millipede hesitated. The old man, Dinorego, had remarked that very day that Maria no longer attended her English lessons. These used to take place at just about sunset and last for an hour each evening. But now, for the last three days, Maria had sat at home by the fire instead of going to the farm as she usually did. Mma-Millipede was hesitant to impart this information to Paulina, as already she looked the picture of despair.

"Look here, my child," she said, firmly. "The man is a newcomer and you can't go jumping to conclusions. Besides, I suspect that Maria has long been in love with Gilbert, only you are not to spread this about."

These words prevented Paulina from giving way completely to despair. She even gossiped quite gaily with Mma-Millipede about trifling matters, then a short while later arose and left for her own home. But Paulina's revelations of her interest in Makhaya caused Mma-Millipede a few hours of anxious thought. Mma-Millipede was of the old school, among whom, to a certain extent, foreigners were still taboo. Also, her experience of men had been a very limited and disastrous one. Most of all she feared that another tragedy would be too much for her impetuous young friend.

"I hope Makhaya is a good man," she said over and over to herself.

Just at this time, Makhaya was trying to avoid a situation at the farm that both exasperated and amused him. To Gilbert, agriculture was a vast, rambling, intricate subject. The slope of the land and even the stones that lay on that land would spark off a thousand speculations in his mind, and there were so few good listeners in the world that Makhaya found himself trapped and almost forced to listen to long discussions on the marvels and wonders of the earth. Not that Makhaya minded. It was a welcome change to be hearing about these things. There was much more than South Africa that he was running away from, and it included everything that he felt was keeping the continent of Africa at a standstill. On the one hand, you felt yourself the persecuted man, and on the other, you so easily fell prey to all the hate-making political ideologies, which seemed to him to be the order of the day. Yet these hate-making ideologies in turn gave rise to a whole new set of retrogressive ideas and retrogressive pride, and it was almost a mania to think that the whole world was against you. And how many pompous, bombastic fools had not jumped on this bandwagon? Yet the very real misery was still there. No matter what kind of fool you made of yourself, people in southern Africa were still oppressed.

At some stage, and in an effort to solve his own dilemma, he decided to strike out on his own. He saw this mass of suffering mankind of which he was a part, but he also saw himself as a separate particle, too, and as time went on he began to stress his own separateness, taking this as a guide that would lead him to clarity of thought in all the confusion. It was rare. It was an uphill task in a part of the world where everyone tended to cling to his or her precious prejudice and tradition, and the act of letting go of it all greatly increased a man's foes. You find yourself throwing blows but weeping at the same time, because of all the people who sit and wail in the darkness, and because of all the fat smug persecutors to whom this wailing is like sweet music, and some inner voice keeps on telling you that your way is right for you, that the process of rising up from the darkness is an intensely personal and private one, and that if you can find a society that leaves the individual to develop freely you ought to choose that society as your home. Makhaya had made the first move along this road but at the same time he was often stricken with guilt. If Joas Tsepe had called him to his face, "a traitor to the African cause", he would have agreed in his heart because he threw most of his blows at Africa and had done so for a long time. Thus when Makhaya met Gilbert, he was almost a drowning man, and this world of facts and scientific speculation seemed so much easier to handle. Therefore Makhaya turned to agriculture for his salvation, and also to Gilbert. And he did this in guilt and fear of his intuitions because they seemed to him to lack any practical solutions as to why so many people could be persecuted by so few and why so many starved while a few had more than they could eat.

Gilbert was a complete contrast to this wavering, ambiguous world in which Makhaya lived. He was first and foremost a practical, down-to-earth kind of man, intent only on being of useful service to his fellow men. There was nothing fanciful in him, yet the workings of his mind often confused and fascinated Makhaya. It was like one gigantic storage house of facts and figures and plans and intuitive judgments and impressions. The wheels kept on turning at such a fast pace that Makhaya never ceased to be amazed at the way Gilbert always spoke in a calm, almost soft tone, while the loud humming of these wheels was almost audible. Gilbert's mind was also like a stop watch. He could abruptly break off a conversation and, ten hours later, pick it up at the exact same point where he had left off. Gilbert prided himself on being an unusually well-informed man. No doubt the sun did too. No doubt the sun knew why the clouds formed and why the wind blew and why the lizards basked in its warmth, and all this immense knowledge made the sun gay and bright, full of trust and affection for mankind. But there were shut-away worlds where the sunlight never penetrated, haunted worlds, full of mistrust and hate, and it was about this side of life that Makhaya was particularly well informed. This sharp contrast in outlook called for a compromise, and Makhaya debated awhile and then gave way. Although manly and independent-minded enough, he found it necessary to say "yes" or merely listen on far too many occasions, and he consoled himself with the thought that he had a lot to learn. In any case, Gilbert's company and friendship disturbed him far less than most people's did, although Gilbert's views on African and world politics were extremely naïve and childlike.

Since poverty was so much a part of his work, Gilbert was fond of expounding on what the British Socialists and the trade union movement had done to alleviate the atrocious living and working conditions of the poor. He several times mentioned his uneasy suspicions of the new Botswana government with its debates on democracy and a tax system that too eagerly encouraged private enterprise.

"Where is all this talk of democracy going to get us, Mack?" he said one day, glumly. "Only a reasonably developed country can afford the time to debate these pros and cons. What we need here is a dictatorship that will feed, clothe and educate a people. I could work well with a dictatorship which says: Look here, Gilbert, fill in this poverty programme."

He looked at Makhaya, half laughing, half in deep earnest. Makhaya returned an almost hostile look.

Not any politics in the world meant anything to him as a stateless person, and every political discussion was a mockery, he felt, of his own helplessness. Since he kept so silent, it forced Gilbert to add, apologetically:

"I'm not saying that the dictator should stay there, forever, Mack. He must eventually give way to the democracy. But in my opinion a dictatorship is the best method for governing a country like this. What do you think?"

Makhaya nearly laughed out loud. Gilbert's statements were an explanation of his own personality. He was a man only impressed by results, and he had been unable to produce these in Botswana the way agricultural experts had produced them in Russia and China. Makhaya wanted to put forward the idea that certain types of socialism might not be suited to African development. Africa had a small population, and it might well be that socialism of every kind was an expedient to solve unwieldly population problems. But his mind swerved away from even this. If a man talked about governments and political systems, he'd soon want to be a part of the whole rotten crew. He preferred to live in the bush.

"Why not leave this country, even Africa, to trial and error?" he said slowly, uncomfortably. "This is only my opinion. I don't think I approve of dictatorships in any form, whether for the good of mankind or not. Even if it is painstakingly slow, I prefer a democracy for Africa, come what may."

Whether this was a satisfactory remark or not, Gilbert never referred to politics again. Makhaya did not care because, more than anything, he hated politics. Perhaps people could be fed after all, and once it came to the time when a man had to die, he might be more proud to count up the number of his fellow men he had helped to live, rather than the number he had bombed into oblivion.

It was this private anxiety to put his life to a useful purpose that made Makhaya an amenable listener to the long agricultural discussions, and since Gilbert had at last found a potential convert to his faith, he often pressed Makhaya into having supper with him. The food was quite often cooked by Maria, who had always been Gilbert's companion at this hour because of the Tswana and English lessons. On the two occasions Makhaya had been present, he had not failed to notice, with his sensitivity to atmosphere, that his presence was deeply resented by Maria, worse still since Gilbert absent-mindedly talked agriculture, overlooking her, whereas at this time the hour was usually spent in loud chatter, arguments and laughter. Makhaya could quite clearly hear these friendly exchanges as his hut was very near that of Gilbert's. They pleased and surprised him, and he came to the conclusion that the aloof Maria had put a great deal of effort into the friendship. To no one else did she condescend to laugh and talk in such a gay, free manner. He understood her temperament, it being very much like his own, and he immediately interpreted the hostility as an inability to admit a stranger into a close relationship. It was this that made Makhaya take walks out into the sunset. But there was also a wide streak of unselfishness in Maria, and she in turn made an elaborate gesture of staying away. It only confused matters and exasperated Makhaya because, for almost three nights after that, Gilbert kept breaking off in the middle of a conversation to say: "I wonder why Maria isn't coming around any more?"

And then he'd stare at Makhaya as though Makhaya had something to do with it.

On the evening that Makhaya brought back the

thornbush seeds, everything came to a head. Makhaya found Gilbert and Pelotona, the permit man, seated around a log fire near Gilbert's hut. He joined them, and for a time the discussion was about salt licks, bonemeal, and fodder which were needed at the cattle ranch. Pelotona lived in a hut on the ranch, and for a year had managed both the ranch and cattle co-operative, being assisted by Gilbert only on cattle trucking days. After a while, Pelotona stood up and left for his home on the ranch.

Noting that Gilbert's mood was silent, reserved and aloof, Makhaya referred to the seeds which he still held in his hand. Gilbert took them and immediately brightened.

"You know," he said. "I noticed the very same thing. I looked it up and found out that the thornbush is an acacia, a branch of the legumes, which includes peas and beans . . ."

And he had that expression on his face when he was about to launch out into the miracles and wonders of nature, but suddenly he broke off and slipped back into a mood of intense, reserved silence. He stared at Makhaya for a while and then said:

"I hope you don't love Maria, too."

So that's what it all came to, Makhaya thought, and smiled. And he just sat there in the shadowy light of the fire and maintained a deliberate silence. It was all none of his business, and he was experienced enough to know that people who reach a deadlock in their emotional relationships often blame this on others. Gilbert simply misinterpreted this silence and stood up abruptly and walked into his hut. Makhaya did the same, with the only exception that Makhaya was at peace in his mind and hugely enjoying himself. He lit a lamp and picked up a book and then lay full length down on the bed to read. Gilbert paced about in his hut for a bit. He was disturbed and unaccountably angry with someone, but his mind refused to acknowledge who it was. After a time he put on a thick blue jersey and walked down to the home of Dinorego.

He found the old man and Maria seated near an outdoor fire. They both looked up at his approach and then maintained an alarmed silence, as they could both see that something was wrong. It wasn't the same Gilbert with that rushing expression of joy on his face, and he walked slowly with his arms folded across his chest. He deliberately ignored Maria and greeted the old man in a quiet voice.

Maria stood up and said in a slightly trembling voice, "Would you like some tea, Gilbert?"

He did not reply but she rushed away into one of the huts merely to get away from this nervous atmosphere and then stood there, trembling from head to foot, unable to reach out for a cup and saucer.

The old man looked at Gilbert solicitously. Whatever was wrong, he was not prepared to go into a panic until he had heard the worst. Dinorego had great faith in his own reasoning ability. It was always there, at the forefront, like a cool waterfall on his thoughts. Gilbert sat down and continued his intense staring into the fire. Eventually the old man asked, "What's the trouble, son?"

Gilbert raised his head and looked at the old man. "I'm going to marry your daughter," he said, quietly.

For once, Dinorego was completely deprived of his speech. Not only that, his ready wit and sound moralizing on every event also deserted him.

"Do you have any objections?" Gilbert persisted, since the old man just stared at him.

"I am trying to put my thoughts together, son," Dinorego said at last. He had expected to hear a forecast about the drought, or that all the farm machinery had broken down, and just right now all that familiar side of Gilbert had been replaced by a man he hardly knew. He looked for a crutch and called out to his daughter. She appeared like a swift shadow and stood just outside the circle of light.

"Do you hear what Gilbert says," he said. "Gilbert says he is going to marry you. Are you agreeable?"

"Yes, Papa," she said.

The world righted itself a bit.

"And when do you intend this marriage to take place, my son?" the old man asked, kindly.

"Tomorrow," Gilbert said.

Dinorego raised his hands in the air, as though saying that the whole business was a bit too much for him.

"As you can see, I am very pleased, my son," he said. "Only . . ." and he turned to Maria. "My child, you must go to Mma-Millipede at once. She will know what to do about the marriage which is to take place tomorrow."

Gilbert stood up and accompanied Maria for a short while along the dark footpath. From where he sat, the old man heard shouts of laughter and arguments, and he sat there smiling to himself, contemplating the mystery of youth. He had never seen any other man survive so much frustration, difficulties and trouble as Gilbert had, and here he was preparing to rush into more. And Gilbert, once Maria had left him, stood at the crossroads near the farm and looked up at the stars and laughed. If the old man really knew, Gilbert's life was simple and uncomplicated. Life to him meant love and work. It meant getting out of the rut and the habitual way of doing things. It was like all the rivers and sunsets and the fish in the rivers and the trees and pathways and sun and wind. But most of all it was work. Because, lack of work meant death. And while he thought of all these things, Gilbert's mind was once more recalled to the workaday world. Those trees—he had forgotten to enlighten Makhaya on the full meaning of the life of the thorn scrub. He turned and swung his way back to the farm.

The lamp still burned in Makhaya's hut and Gilbert knocked and, without waiting for a reply, pushed the door open and walked in. Makhaya balanced the book on his chest, glanced up briefly and noticed the excitement that shone in his friend's eyes. This friend grabbed a chair, sat down and took up the conversation at the point where it had been abruptly broken off.

"The thornbush is most definitely an acacia, Mack," he said. "Now, the twining around of the seed-pod is a device for ejecting the seeds when they are ripe, so that they will be flung away from the parent plant. This also explains why the thornbush is able to encroach so rapidly on cultivated land. It's the toughest little plant I know, but the goats are browsing it to death. Did you know that goats are natural browsers?"

"No," said Makhaya, smiling inwardly.

"Goats prefer shrubs to grass, however lush and sweet," he said. "But they will eat grass when it is in seed. Much of northern Africa is desert today because the goats destroyed the thornbush. I've nothing against the goats, you know. Without their meat and milk we'd all starve in Golema Mmidi, but we'll have to do something about controlling their eating habits, one of these days."

Gilbert sat for a moment in deep thought, no doubt trying to invent new eating habits for the goats, but there was too much he had to keep a tab on tonight. His own emotional life kept intruding into his scientific speculations, and he suspected himself of having committed some grievous crime. It was unthinkable that he had precipitated himself into marriage through jealousy of Makhaya, and he was trying to work around this thought before springing the surprise.

"You know," he said, in a burst of generosity. "I'd meant to tell you this some time ago, Mack. You're Kipling's 'Thousandth Man'. Do you know the poem?"

"No," Makhaya said again, and it was an effort for him to control his laughter. He felt he knew what was coming next.

"Somehow I knew this the day you stepped into Golema Mmidi," Gilbert said. "And it's just today that everything's clear to me . . ."

He quoted a few lines from the poem:

> *"One man in a thousand," Solomon said,*
> *"Will stick more close than a brother:*
> *And it's worth while seeking him half your days,*
> *If you find him before the other . . ."*

But Makhaya had a few reservations about Mr. Kipling's sweeping statements. It was just a chance that had brought him to Golema Mmidi, and it was only chance and luck that operated in his destiny.

"I suppose you mean by that that you're no longer mad at me," he observed, dryly. "You nearly bit my head off not so long ago."

"It's not you I was mad at, Mack," Gilbert said. "It was Maria. You've no idea how she's made me run in circles for three years. Now it's all ended so easily, I can't believe it myself. I don't know why I never thought of going to Dinorego in the first place. You know what he said: 'Do you hear, Maria? Gilbert says he's going to marry you. Do you agree?' And all she said was, 'Yes, Papa.' Just that, after saying a thousand different things to me. So, I thought she'd change her mind and I said we'd get married tomorrow."

By this time, Maria had already reached the home of Mma-Millipede. She found her alone, reading the Tswana version of the Bible.

She was a little apprehensive as the door was pushed open and Maria stepped in, especially as a visit from Maria was rare, and then the child just stood there, a little breathless, flustered and tongue-tied.

"Batho! What's the matter, my child?" she asked anxiously.

"Papa sent me to tell you I am to marry Gilbert tomorrow."

"But why the haste?" said Mma-Millipede, quite taken aback.

Maria sat down. "There's no haste, Mama," she said, in her earnest way. "It's I who have delayed matters. Gilbert has asked me to marry him for three years."

"Does Papa agree?" the old woman asked.

Maria nodded and Mma-Millipede smiled inwardly, pleased that all her conjectures were at last confirmed. But curiosity overcame her and she said, "Three years is a long time to delay a marriage, my child. Gilbert might have become impatient and run away to England; then not only would you have lost him, but we too."

Maria stared at the old woman with small withdrawn eyes and shook her head a little helplessly. How could Mma-Millipede expect to understand all the complications of life? She placed one small straight hand on the table, a way she had of showing that sentiment should always be separated from facts.

"Gilbert is a man with many strange ways," she said crisply. "A person has to get used to these strange ways. For some time now he has kept a lizard in the house whom he treats as a person and which is now accustomed to being spoken to like a person. Its name is Skin. Each night it is put down beside the lamp to have a meal off the insects that gather there. Also, I have often seen it asleep on the pillow, like a child, with its legs spread out. Gilbert does not live in this world but in some world about which I know nothing."

Mma-Millipede nodded her head slowly, with an expression on her face which clearly said: Oh, People, is that what foreign men are like?

"Are you sure you want to marry, my child?" she asked, kindly.

The young girl shrugged, helplessly. "I don't know my own mind, Mama," she said, in despair. "I don't know what I want. You must help me."

"But you help yourself with your understanding, my child," the old woman said. "As you know, we all live in a world that is full of danger. If a person cannot see this, he must be protected from the danger."

Maria stared meditatively at the table. "I thought so too, Mama." she said slowly. "I don't care about myself, but nothing must harm Gilbert."

These words suddenly relieved Mma-Millipede of the burden of sentiment that was clouding her practical mind.

"There is so much to do," she said. "And so little time. We have to give a party. How often is there a wedding? Once in a blue moon. More likely it is death or ailments that bring people together. Two or three goats will have to be slaughtered and some chickens for high diet. I am out of rice. Has Papa any rice?"

"We have plenty, Mama," the young girl said.

"And what about a pretty dress in which to get married?" Mma-Millipede said. "Never mind, we shall buy it tomorrow."

She sat for a moment, ticking off the items in her mind. The goats would have to be slaughtered early in the morning and then hung up to drain. No doubt she would have to accompany her old friend to the wedding ceremony, and there was only one other woman in the village capable of managing the party arrangements while she was away—Paulina Sebeso. She stood up, searched for an old jacket, and, accompanied by Maria, walked to the home of her friend, Paulina.

They passed the farm and the lamp still burned in Makhaya's hut, and the two men still chatted like ancient blood brothers. They passed another home where the old man sat, staring pensively into the fire, contemplating the twists and turns of a long life which might end any day now, he thought, since his last and youngest child was about to marry. But if Dinorego thought about death near his softly glowing fire, Paulina Sebeso thought about life and how to have it more abundantly. And the bright crackling flames of her fire danced upward into the black sky. She sprang to her feet as the old woman and the young woman approached.

"I have a surprise," Mma-Millipede said.

And once she heard what it was, Paulina Sebeso turned round and too vigorously pushed a log into the fire. She did this to cover up her confusion, and the disturbed fire sent sparks in all directions. Paulina was unashamedly joyful that a stroke of luck had removed her deadliest competitor.

Chapter 7

Early the next morning, at the home of Mma-Millipede, bedlam reigned. The women of the village were there, and two goats, slaughtered and skinned, hung up by the feet from a tree to drain off the excess blood. Until the blood flowed down to a trickle, there was nothing much for the women to do except stand as close to each other as possible and create the most ear-splitting din. This whole process is sometimes known as talking, but it has been said that it is only Basotho women who outmatch Batswana women at this art; that is, you stand about a foot away from your companion, heave up your chest, puff up the side veins of the neck and then let all you have inside you come out, full blast. Somehow you laugh at the same time, and unusual this sound is too, as though all the glass in the world were being hurled into a deep pit and shrieking in agony. This noise attracted all the goats in the village to the home of Mma-Millipede, for they knew from long experience that it was the signal for a thousand potato peels to fall on the ground. They added to the din by fighting, pushing and bleating for the best positions. And, of course, Botswana is one of the greatest tea-drinking countries in the world, so that the clatter of over a hundred teacups added the final touch to the shattering symphony.

Everyone had brought along a little something to put into the pot. Mostly it was potatoes, and these little gifts were tied up in gay blue, red and yellow checkered cloths and hung from the waists of the women, and these checkered splashes of colour swayed about as they talked. At a sign from Paulina, an abrupt and deathly silence fell on the gathering. A few women moved forward and sliced out the hard fat that had surrounded the intestines of the animals and which, when heated, melted down into oil. This fat was divided into equal portions and placed in two large iron pots which stood near the fire. On top of this fat they poured small packets of curry powder. Another group of women advanced on the slaughtered goats and, within a short space of time, sliced away all the meat, leaving behind the bony skeleton. The meat, fat, and curry powder then boiled away in big pots. Everyone moved over to small wooden tables, on the top of each of which was placed a basin containing water; and then, with strained, absorbed faces, the women peeled the potatoes, tossing them one by one into the basins. Even the goats quieted down, absorbed in munching the peels with their small dainty mouths.

A shrill high-pitched voice, the owner of which was carefully submerged in the group, broke the silence. "I am wondering about the foreigner who has recently come to the farm," it said.

Since everyone had been wondering too, everyone kept quiet.

"Who knows if he is married?" the shrill voice persisted.

"Why don't you direct your questions to Paulina Sebeso?" a voice at the farthest end of the crowd shouted, and then, with a hint of sarcasm, added, "After all, she's the big brains around here."

Everyone turned and stared at Paulina, and she had caught the slight edge of sarcasm and was angry yet remained calm.

"I know nothing," she said, in a deliberately flat voice.

"But you have eyes, Paulina Sebeso," the sarcastic one continued. "You must have noticed that the foreigner is very handsome."

Paulina turned and stared at her tormentor. The owner of the sarcastic voice was Grace Sebina, a rough, wild, promiscuous woman. They had been at loggerheads for some time.

"If your eyes chase all the men, Grace Sebina," she said crisply, "please don't put them on me."

All the women stared at each other in shock. It wasn't polite to call a prostitute a prostitute in black and white terms.

"You don't have to be so rude, Paulina Sebeso," one of the older women said, reprovingly. "Grace Sebina is portraying our own thoughts. We all think the foreigner is handsome. We only want to know if you think the same."

Paulina stood there and bit on her tongue, too late, while they all stared at her innocently. It was bait-talk. It had been planned. They all had permanent lovers or husbands while Paulina Sebeso had none, and even a tradition was forming about her. A few men had said she was too bossy. Then they all said it, overlooking the fact that they were wilting, effeminate shadows of men who really feared women. Things went along smoothly as long as all the women pretended to be inferior to this spineless species. The women had been lying to themselves for so long in their sexual frustration that they would not admit the real reason why Paulina dominated them all was because she was the kind of woman who could not lie to men. They followed the leadership of Paulina because she was so daring and different. It would have upset their world to have Paulina find a man she could get along with. They were determined to keep her trapped in a frustration far greater than their own. In fact, on several occasions, this powerful little clique had stepped in and with a few poisonous, cunning words destroyed tentative friendships. The innocent glances were therefore a challenge. Would she make a bid for the foreigner? And if so, was she prepared to face the consequences?

Paulina turned and stirred one of the pots with a big wooden stick. It wasn't the women and their intriguing she feared but the untrustworthiness of men with no strength or moral values. It was as though a whole society had connived at producing a race of degenerate men by stressing their superiority in the law and overlooking how it affected them as individuals. These things Paulina felt intuitively, but had not thought out in a coherent form. Strangely enough, she now began to look with hope upon the event of the previous evening, when Makhaya had spurned her gesture of friendship. If he had walked straight into her yard on her invitation, she reasoned, might he not too have walked into every other woman's yard?

So when the older, reproving woman said, "We see, Paulina Sebeso, you have no words to defend yourself?" she turned round and smiled.

"What can I say, Mama," she said. "I have seen the foreigner about in the village. It seems to me he has big ears, and I don't see how a man with such big ears can be handsome."

The women turned and looked at each other with meaningful glances as much as to say: We are not so easily fooled by you, Paulina Sebeso.

Paulina was not like the women of Golema Mmidi, although she had been born into their kind of world and fed on the same diet of thin maize porridge by a meek, repressed, dull-eyed mother. But even as a small child she kept on putting her nose into everything. "What's this, Mama?" she'd say, with a face screwed up with fun and mischief. She was so lively and meddlesome that her mother constantly kept a little switch nearby, and it was quite a common sight in her village to see Paulina racing through the thornbush with her mother hard on her heels, waving the switch. Because of this early practice, once she attended school she became one of the fastest runners on sports competition days. Her athletic ability had ensured her more education than most of the women in the village, and it was only the prospect of a secure and stable marriage that had made her discontinue attending school. But throughout her life she had retained her fresh, lively curiosity and ability to enter an adventure, head first. It was all this that really distinguished her from the rest of the women, even though her circumstances and upbringing were no different from theirs.

She had travelled a longer way, too, on the road of life, as unexpected suffering always makes a human being do, and yet her thoughts were as uncertain and intangible as the blue smoke of the fires which unfurled into the still winter air and disappeared like vapour. Caught up in this pensive mood, she hardly saw basin after basin of potatoes being pitched into the huge pots, yet she continued to stir the food with quick vigorous thrusts of the wooden spoon, and she hardly heard the women chattering about the marriage ceremony, which was taking place at that moment in the untidy office of George Appleby-Smith. (George, like the women, felt it to be an ordinary and natural outcome of events, because everything the unusual Gilbert did seemed to be harmonious and acceptable like the sunrise and sunsets. George had only added a little drama and humour of his own. His office had not been swept out for some days, and he had kept the wedding party waiting while, with a straight expressionless face, he swept the room out.)

"I say, Paulina Sebeso," one of the women said, "you're letting the chickens burn."

Paulina started and poured a little water into a

smaller pot in which two chickens were roasting in their own fat, and for a time, the chatter of the women imposed itself on the tangled wisps of her thoughts. . . .

"But I must say the daughter of Dinorego is a lucky devil," someone said enviously. "From now on she will live in comfort, as white men know how to make money, not like our men who don't like work."

"Do you suppose she had this comfort foremost in mind?" someone else asked.

"You can't tell with Maria," the other replied. "She's too clever."

Since Paulina also shared this envy of Maria's strange, unfathomable personality and was guilty about it, she turned on the speakers, wrathfully, "I don't like people to discuss a person who is not present."

"Goodness! Paulina Sebeso," one of the speakers said with an injured air. "You are in a cross mood today. Are you perhaps pregnant?"

But Paulina's reply was drowned in shrieks of laughter, and even Paulina herself stood there laughing in confusion at herself. Many strange moods possessed her this day, as though, through some premonition, she was being warned that her whole way of life was about to change.

The change itself was to be a devious, subtle one, the threads of which were woven by three people who were to walk into the yard a few hours later: Gilbert, Mma-Millipede, and Makhaya. Of the three it was only Makhaya who was vitally necessary to her existence. Mma-Millipede's spur-of-the-moment wedding party for everyone drew together the first few strands, which in turn were to draw in hundreds of other strands, affecting the whole future pattern of life in Golema Mmidi. But it was all in the air that day and was in part responsible for Paulina's changeable moods, her pensiveness and unfamiliar uncertainty.

She was relieved, therefore, when at noon she stepped back from the cooking pots and seated herself on a stool in the shadow of a hut. A group of women, who had been idle, stepped up to the pots, getting ready to supervise the dishing up of the food when the wedding party returned.

Shortly after this, the five farm workers and Pelotona, the permit man, walked into the yard, followed a little later by Mma-Millipede, Dinorego, and Maria. Maria looked much put out by being the centre of attention for the day, because she was essentially a quiet and humble personality. It all made her pretty, serious face more serious than usual, and she was at pains to conceal herself behind the ample figure of Mma-Millipede. Not even her new frock of pale blue cotton, sprigged with small pale pink roses, could boost Maria's morale. The women of the village also put on constrained masks as they walked about serving the food in silence. They only let themselves go when they were a group together with no men present.

After a slight delay, Gilbert and Makhaya also walked into the yard absorbed in a conversation. At least, Gilbert was doing the talking and Makhaya the listening. Since she had only waited for the appearance of Makhaya, Paulina looked up and stared at him in a still, intent, almost dispassionate way. She noted how he never once looked at the face of the speaker but kept wrapped up in himself and walked as though he was a single, separate and aloof entity. And yet at the same time he concentrated so intensely on what was being said to him that he seemed to have established an invisible bond between himself and the speaker. Then Gilbert seemed to say something that indicated the end of the conversation and, picking up a hand-carved stool, walked over and sat down on the right side of Mma-Millipede, who had Maria sitting on her left. Makhaya, in turn, looked around the gathering with a slight expression of surprise on his face, as if his absorption in Gilbert's conversation had made him unaware of his surroundings. Paulina's heart turned over at this, and she bent her head and smiled to herself.

The old man, Dinorego, touched Makhaya on the arm and indicated a vacant seat next to him. Makhaya sat down.

"You know, son," Dinorego said confidingly, "I thought the day I met you: 'Well, here is a most suitable man to marry my daughter.' Today, I cannot recover from my surprise, although I am very pleased that she is married to Gilbert. It means he will make his home here and we shall progress."

Makhaya merely laughed in reply, especially at the latter part of the old man's speech. Moralizing seemed to be Dinorego's speciality.

"And what about you, son?" the old man continued. "Might you not like to marry here too?"

Makhaya turned his head and looked at the old man, directly, half-amused, half-serious.

"Most men want to achieve great victories," he said. "But I am only looking for a woman."

The old man nodded his head profoundly, but at the same time he sensed snags in that simple statement. Makhaya appeared to him too complicated a man to have such straightforward desires.

"Might she be very educated or might she not be educated, son?" he asked.

"I know what I want, Papa," Makhaya said quietly. "Because I've had so much of what I did not want."

The old man said nothing but stared thoughtfully into the distance. There were things in Makhaya he would never understand because his own environment was one full of innocence. The terrors of rape, murder and bloodshed in a city slum, which was Makhaya's background, were quite unknown to Dinorego, but he felt in Makhaya's attitude and utterances a horror of life, and it was as though he was trying to flee this horror and replace it with innocence, trust, and respect. In many ways, Gilbert's background was much closer to that of Dinorego's than was Makhaya's, because it contained this same innocence and a lack of understanding of evil. Still, Dinorego was an old man, governed by his own strange rules, and in the short space of time he had known him, he felt a closer bond with Makhaya, the way God usually feels towards the outcast beggar rolling in the dust.

"You must approach my friend Mma-Millipede," Dinorego said at last. "She will enjoy your conversation. She may also help you to find the woman you seek, as she knows the heart of everyone."

Two women came up and handed the men plates of roast chicken, with rice and roast potatoes, which they carried on a tray. Then they moved over to Mma-Millipede, Gilbert and Maria and also served them. Gilbert took his plate and set it down on the ground before him. Just at that moment he had an urgent matter to discuss with Mma-Millipede and the food could wait. He looked at Mma-Millipede anxiously. Would she be able to help him? he asked.

Mma-Millipede turned her face towards Gilbert and smiled. She adored him, as she identified him with her own love of mankind.

"You know there is nothing I would not do for you, my son," she said.

But at the same time she calmly started eating and pointed at his plate, indicating that he should do the same. "If you don't eat," she explained, "the ants will soon invade your plate."

Thus Gilbert was forced to delay his urgent proposal. Mma-Millipede in the meantime noticed the predicament of her friend, Paulina Sebeso, who seemed to have her big, dark eyes glued on the face of Makhaya, and so intent was she on staring that she seemed to have forgotten herself completely. Mma-Millipede felt acute distress.

My friend is going to make a fool of herself over the man, she thought.

Over the years, Mma-Millipede had traced two distinct relationships women had with men in her country. The one was a purely physical relationship. It caused no mental breakdown and was free and casual, each woman having six or seven lovers, including a husband as well. The other was more serious and more rare. It could lead to mental breakdown and suicide on the part of the woman, because, on the one hand, it assumed that the man was worthy of adoration, while in reality he was full of shocks and disappointments; and on the other, this adoration assumed the proportions of a daily diet of a most dangerous nature. Since Mma-Millipede had to sew the funeral garments, she had come to dread this latter type of relationship and gave preference, against her conscience, to the former. Surely, she reasoned, it was far better to have a country of promiscuous women than a country of dead women? Mma-Millipede looked over at Makhaya. No matter how hard she tried, she could not form a judgment on his character because of her inhibition about foreign men. She sighed deeply.

She put her plate down, momentarily debating ways in which she could question Gilbert about Makhaya's character. These questions would have to be very subtle and not reveal her real interest, which was to protect and advise her friend, Paulina Sebeso. At the same time Gilbert also put down his plate and turned towards Mma-Millipede.

The problem was this, Gilbert explained. He wanted the women of the village, first and foremost, to start producing cash crops which would be marketed co-operatively through the farm. The idea was to get capital in hand which would open up the way for purchasing fertilizers, seed and the equipment necessary to increase food production in Golema Mmidi. Once people had enough to eat, other problems like better housing, water supplies and good education for the children could be tackled. Now, said Gilbert, one of the easiest and most profitable cash crops to grow was Turkish tobacco. If each woman cultivated a small plot of Turkish tobacco, harvested and cured it herself, and if it were all marketed co-operatively, the profits could then be spread out to good purpose. Could Mma-Millipede persuade the women to attend lessons at the farm on how to cultivate Turkish tobacco and how to build a curing and drying shed?

Mma-Millipede nodded her head vigorously. Like Gilbert, she had vision and she clearly saw the wondrous benefits that would accrue to the people of Golema Mmidi.

"Are you going to give the women instruction, my son?" she asked.

"No, not me, but Makhaya," he said. "I've specially asked him to accept responsibility for this side of the work. The farm itself takes up all my time, Mma-Millipede, but I'm anxious that it should not progress beyond the living conditions of the people of Golema Mmidi. Both have to grow together. I chose Makhaya for this side of the work because I think he will enjoy imparting knowledge to people."

Mma-Millipede sat rigidly silent on receiving this news, yet her mind began to work at a rapid and alert pace. The only woman who would have the courage to persuade the other women to attend lessons at the farm was Paulina Sebeso, and having to approach Makhaya at a closer level, in the company of other women, might help her friend to put this sudden adoration on a sounder basis. But Mma-Millipede still needed a little information in order to be able to advise her friend on how she should conduct herself without coming to grief.

"Is Makhaya a man of good character?" she asked innocently.

Gilbert stared at her in surprise. Why, all his future plans depended on Makhaya. Not only that, he had had no way of starting the plan of this new venture until Makhaya had arrived. He had no way of explaining to Mma-Millipede the real subtleties of his relationship with Makhaya, that he was someone he now leaned on heavily for courage to push ahead with his ideas. Gilbert had long known that his survival in Golema Mmidi depended on many complicated factors, one of these being Chief Sekoto. It did not take him long to find out that Chief Sekoto did not care deeply about development projects and that he, Gilbert, was the medium through which Chief Sekoto inflicted revenge on his brother Matenge. Gilbert had been fearful of being critical about the African way of life, which seemed to him a deadly, chilling society which kept out anything new and strange. It was as though people looked at each other all the time, questioning themselves: Am I exactly the same as my neighbour? The fear was to differ from the next man, and he could see it in so many little ways, even in Golema Mmidi—the way a great scientific discovery like the drought-resistant millet meant nothing against traditional prejudice. Would the superior Motswana turn overnight into a Kalahari bushman if he ate millet? He seemed to think so, irrespective of the fact that millet was just an innocent food which an "inferior" tribe had developed a liking for. This damned millet, even though fields and fields of it could be grown in this country. Of course, he had

Dinorego, who copied him in everything, but once Makhaya had come to the village a lot of his silent tortures had blown away in the wind. It mattered very much to Gilbert to have as a friend a man who looked as black as everyone else and yet was not at all a part of these chilling group attitudes. And there was more to Makhaya's personality than that—a gentleness that communicated itself as a strength and gave peace to others, a complete lack of fear, and a background of persecution which made it so easy for him to identify himself with the rags and tatters of the poor. But there was more still, there was more, and he bent his head searching around for some coherent explanation of his liking for Makhaya. He grasped the first thought that flashed across his mind:

"Makhaya is one of the most truthful men on earth," he said. "You can depend on him. Besides, he is a real friend to me."

Mma-Millipede was very moved by this declaration. "Gilbert," she said, seriously. "I think I accept your word. Tomorrow I'll send a friend to the farm who will discuss the matter with you. I think she will also bring along her friends. Excuse me, I shall approach her right away."

Mma-Millipede arose and walked slowly in the direction of Paulina Sebeso. It was most urgent to her future schemes that she prevent Paulina from staring any longer at Makhaya like a felled ox. But Mma-Millipede's sudden rising had left Maria without her shelter, and all at once she looked like a fragile wild flower, about to be blown away in the wind. Gilbert turned his head and looked at her, feeling strangely uncertain that he was really married to this changeable, unpredictable woman. There were two women in her—one was soft and meditative and the other was full of ruthless common sense, and these two uncongenial personalities clashed and contradicted each other all the time. He wasn't ever sure if Maria was in need of his constant protection or whether everyone was really superfluous to this still, midnight world of quiet self-absorption in which she lived. She was in one of her self-absorbed moods right now. He moved over to Mma-Millipede's vacant seat, took one of her hands in his, and bent his head teasingly near her face.

"What are you thinking about, Pal?" he asked.

She raised her head and stared at him steadily, and that steady stare always meant fireworks. "Are you going back to England one day?" she asked abruptly.

The edges of his eyes crinkled up in amusement. "We might have to," he said.

Maria placed her free hand straight out on her knee, indicating she had made a rule from which she was not going to budge. "You will have to go back to England by yourself," she said, flatly. "I shall not live in England with you."

"You mean you don't love me, Pal?" he asked, pretending despair.

"It's not that, Gilbert," she said crisply. "I won't feel free in England."

And a lot of funny things occurred to Gilbert all at once. Of late, the Joas Tsepe crowd had been issuing blood-curdling pamphlets about the volunteers in Batswana, calling them the unemployed of Britain who had come here to cheat the Batswana out of jobs. If the Joas Tsepes overthrew the government by force, as they were always threatening to do, he would be frozen out of the country. He had not felt free in England either, at least not in the upper middle class background into which he had been born, where the women all wore pearls, and everyone was nice and polite to everyone, and you could not tell friend from foe behind the polite brittle smiles; and if your mother's brother bought his wife a mansion, your mother had to have a mansion too or threaten to commit suicide, and then your mother almost did commit suicide a few years after you were born because all the polite women kept on remarking about how you were such a big-boned lad with an ungainly walk and didn't somehow quite fit.

"You really ought to send the child to dancing school, Elizabeth," they all said. "It's sure to correct his walk."

And his stupid, neurotic mother had sent him to dancing school, and the dancing teacher had sent him home in tears because he had given her a belly punch when she had tried to force him to dance, and since the belly punch had worked on the dancing teacher, he also tried out a few on his mother; and the way it is with neurotic women, she soon invented a number of excuses as to why it was he lived almost the year round in a tent among the trees. The bird had trailed tiny footpaths through the dense-white, dew-wet grass on summer mornings, and the leaden winter skies had looked like great swathes of eternity which were there to stay, forever and forever. But he found out that there was no eternity: only the ever changing pattern of life. And it was from his tent among the trees that he had learned his humility and tenderness, and that this humility was not compatible with the great causes of the world but only with some work done, preferably in a quiet backwater like Golema Mmidi.

Still, from some unknown quarter, Gilbert had acquired a number of conservative ideas about married life—like it was the man who was the boss and who laid down rules.

"You're not Dinorego's daughter any more," he said to Maria, in a quiet threatening voice. "You're my wife now and you have to do as I say. If I go back to England, you go there too."

The woman of common sense retreated rapidly

before the threat, and the other woman softly contradicted her, "I did not say I won't obey you, Gilbert. I only wanted to find out what was on your mind."

But thoughts of home, of England, had struck Gilbert with a sudden, deep loneliness. The feel of the still, blue, Botswana winter day had the same feel of the February days in England when the snowdrops came out. He stood up and pulled Maria by the hand, and together they walked away far into the bush where the scarlet and gold birds talked to each other in low, soft tones.

Chapter

Paulina Sebeso awoke early the next morning. She was in a slightly unbalanced mood, and the clear, sparkling light of the heady winter morning added to her intoxication. On the previous day at the wedding party Mma-Millipede had told her certain things that had made her heart drunk with joy. She had had to struggle to concentrate on the details of the tobacco growing project, and Mma-Millipede, noticing this, had added a number of stern warnings: You must above all control yourself, my friend. You must pretend you are interested in the tobacco and give yourself time to study the man. Foreign men need studying, even though I accept Gilbert's word that he is a good man.

Not long after Paulina had lit her small outdoor fire to make tea and heat washing water, ten other women walked briskly into the yard. Twenty more had been willing to join the tobacco growing project, but they first had to get the permission of their husbands. The ten women who joined Paulina were agog with excitement. They seated themselves around the jutting mud foundation of one of Paulina's huts and ragged her about not having washed yet, nor made tea.

"Goodness! The tobacco won't run away," Paulina said gaily, and she splashed some water into a basin.

It was always like this. Any little thing was an adventure. They were capable of pitching themselves into the hardest, most sustained labour with perhaps the same joy that society women in other parts of the world experience when they organize fêtes or tea parties. No men ever worked harder than Botswana women, for the whole burden of providing food for big families rested with them. It was their sticks that thrashed the corn at harvesting time and their winnowing baskets that filled the air for miles and miles around with the dust of husks, and they often, in addition to broadcasting the seed when the early rains fell, took over the tasks of the men and also ploughed the land with oxen.

As always, when women left their own homes for the day, they took with them their food supplies in the bright checkered cloths, and these they undid now. One of the women stood up and collected small helpings of tea leaves and powdered milk from each bundle, and then both the powdered milk and tea leaves were poured at the same time into the boiling water. By the time Paulina emerged, dressed and washed, with her small daughter, tea was ready and poured. Also a plate of flat, hard sorghum cakes was handed around. Paulina took a few of the cakes off the plate and wrapped them in a cloth and handed this to the child, instructing her, as it was school holidays, to go and spend the day at the home of Mma-Millipede. Then they all drank the tea with clouds of vapour rising up from the mugs into the cold air. Each woman then carefully rinsed her mug and tied it up once again in the checkered cloth. They arose and walked in a brisk, determined group to the farm, Paulina taking the lead as she always and automatically did.

They found the farm yard deserted, but tractors whirred out in the fields as the winter ploughing was still in progress. Maria, however, emerged from one of the huts and waved and smiled. They hardly recognized her. She seemed quite changed, and not one of the women could ever recall when Maria had ever looked anything but pensive. They all fell on her, teasing her mercilessly and talking all at once.

"Hmm, married life changes a person," they said.

"Tell us! How does he kiss? Come on, tell us!"

Maria waited until the uproar had died down, smiling in her secret way all the while. Then she raised one hand.

"You must all wait until Makhaya comes off the land," she said. "He is taking lessons in tractor ploughing, as this is new to him. He will be here quite soon."

"Where is the husband?" they asked.

"He's working in the office," she said.

The women again settled themselves around the jutting mud foundation of the hut, and the tea-drinking ritual was once more repeated, amidst much laughter and jokes about married life to discomfort Maria.

They had just tucked away their mugs when Makhaya appeared. He walked to his own hut to remove a blue overall and then approached the women. They all stood up and said, "Goodday, sir," together. Makhaya paused, looked at them, smiled and said, "Good-morning," in a friendly, natural voice as though he was long accustomed to receiving people as his guests. Then he said, "Follow me," and led the way to a part of the yard where a small plot of tobacco had been cultivated.

The experimental plot was forty-eight square yards. It had been scaled down to this size by Gilbert, as being the most manageable area for each individual woman to cultivate in her own yard. But one hundred such plots were needed to produce the quantity of tobacco that would be profitable to market, and this also meant that a hundred or more women had to become involved in the project.

The small group of women, including Paulina, at first felt a little inhibited. They were unaccustomed to a man speaking to them as an equal. They stood back awhile, with uneasy expressions, but once it struck them that he paid no attention to them as women, they also forgot he was a man and became absorbed in following his explanations. And this was really part of the magic of Makhaya's personality. He could make people feel at ease. He could change a whole attitude of mind merely in the way he raised his hand or smiled. But he never exerted himself, seeming to leave it to the other party with whom he was communicating to do all the exerting and changing.

He stood and pointed to the plot on which a foot high of tobacco was already growing. It was growing on a gently sloping mound, and this had been created by building up the soil in a heap, the same as when one constantly pitches ash in one place. The need for this mound was to assist in draining the soil, as well-drained soil was needed for the tobacco. He also broke off a tobacco leaf and explained that the very dark blue-green colouring meant that it was an unripe leaf, but once the leaf had matured it changed to a pale, light olive green.

He stopped talking awhile and turned and looked at the women to ask them a few direct questions. The experimental plot would be ready for harvesting in about three months' time. If the women harvested, cured and dried this first batch together, they would gain the necessary experience and be able that much sooner to cultivate, harvest and process their own tobacco. Therefore, it had been decided by him and Gilbert that the first tobacco curing shed be built in the yard of someone who lived nearest the farm.

"Who lives near the farm?" he asked.

The women all turned and looked at Paulina Sebeso. Makhaya also followed the direction of their glance, and a faint, quizzical expression flitted across his face, as though he knew the woman but could not remember under what circumstances he had met her. Certainly, the gaudy-hued skirt was familiar.

Certainly, he remembered the big, bold eyes. Paulina bent her head in alarm and embarrassment.

"I live near the farm," she muttered.

It was only when they had collected the equipment and walked in the direction of the sunset house that Makhaya recalled the brief incident of two nights ago when a small girl had approached him and touched his hand. He was very fond of children, and as they walked into the yard he turned to Paulina and said, "Where's the child?"

"She's at the home of Mma-Millipede," Paulina replied, but she averted her head, as the unexpected question made her feel strangely vulnerable and exposed.

They set down the equipment for building the shed—pickaxes, spades, tar matting, and pitch—and Makhaya walked about the yard looking for a suitable site. In a secluded corner of the yard he stumbled upon a gigantic operation. It was the work of the little girl. She was in the process of building a model village, all carved out of mud. There were mud goats, mud cattle, mud huts and mud people, and grooved little footpaths for them all to walk on. He stood staring at it for some time, a look of pure delight on his face. Then he turned and chose a site as far removed as possible from this sanctuary of genius, and with lengths of string marked out the shallow foundation for the tobacco curing and drying shed.

The women, with pickaxes and spades, scraped out the foundation. The plan of the shed itself in no way resembled the instructions sent to Gilbert by the tobacco research station, as the curing sheds too had been scaled down to a measurement of ten feet by ten feet and were to be built with materials that were easily available in Golema Mmidi—like lots of mud. Makhaya divided a twenty-foot square into two chambers. One was to be a closed shed, with no of Africa, and the world stood still because of this. Makhaya deviated slightly from this pattern as he was born with a natural inclination for his own company. Thus, Gilbert's scientific outlook was a welcome alternative to him.

He felt, too, that all the tensions, jealousies, frustrations, and endless petty bickering which make up the sum total of all human relationships were in reality unnecessary. This belief was necessary to his own survival, as the desire to retaliate in a violent way against all human selfishness and greed was a powerful urge in him. He found himself, over this period, beginning to combine the two—the good in Gilbert with the good in his own society. Perhaps he did so because he needed to save himself. Some part of him was even fearful that he was being mocked by the gods, and that one day he would find himself pitched back into the nightmare over which he had had no control, just as he had had no control over the living processes which had created him, Makhaya, a man with a black skin, which in turn made men with differently coloured skins jar the quiet and peace of his being and allow him no peace, night or day, to live with a natural part of his body. He suspected that Botswana society had its own merry-go-round, as he had seen from the behaviour and attitudes of Matenge and Joas Tsepe, but he did not have a stake in Botswana society. He did not want a stake in any man's society, and that's why Gilbert and his ideas appealed to him so deeply.

What else could a man do, except seek a manageable life? What else could he, Makhaya, do, except wait here a bit until he lost his hate? It was he, Makhaya, the individual, who was seeking his own living life because he was fearful of the living death a man could be born into. In the meanwhile it seemed to him, for his own private needs, that he should free himself of hatred and concentrate his mind on the details of life in Golema Mmidi.

This life was indeed a full one and, for a beginning, a very pleasant and manageable one. Two weeks after the first tobacco curing and drying shed had been built, one hundred and fifty women joined the tobacco growing project. This meant that a number of sheds could be built, simultaneously, on one day, as the women were now organized by Paulina Sebeso into small work groups. They were able to copy the pattern of the first shed with ease, and if Makhaya's blue overalled person was all about the village, it was to help with the construction of the drying racks, which were a complicated affair worked on a collapsible pulley system. The old man Dinorego joined Makhaya in this work. After a few days, Makhaya left this job completely to the old man and started work on small dams which were to be a source of extra water supply. It was too risky to depend on rainfall alone to give the tobacco project a good start, Gilbert reasoned. Who knew when the drought would break, and already the one farm borehole was heavily strained with having to supply the whole village with good drinking water, plus sustaining the cattle in the ranch.

The dams were to be built on each homestead and they were for the purpose of trapping whatever storm water might rush along the ground during the brief rainy season. They were to be pits, blasted out with dynamite to a depth of seven feet and a width of fifteen feet by fifteen feet. Their capacity would be eight thousand gallons of storm water. The bottom of these pits had to be lined with three layers of mud and polythene and the sides to be supported with sandy, concrete-filled plastic bags. In each case a deep furrow was to be dug to catch the runoff storm water and lead it into the dam. Again, the materials were simple and the costs kept low. The polythene was to be on the farm account until expenses could be deducted from the co-operative sale of the tobacco. Dynamite was commonly used to blast out pit toilets, as water-flush cisterns were almost unknown in this waterless country.

So, almost the day long, Golema Mmidi rocked to the blast of dynamite charges, and huge quantities of earth and rock were hurled high into the air. Makhaya, who buried and set off the charges, was often near enough to be splattered by rock and earth. He liked the drama and the irony, for not so very long ago he had come out of jail for wanting to use this very dynamite against the enemies of human dignity. It was like a self-mockery, this splattering rock and earth, to realize that he was indeed powerless to change an evil and that there were millions and millions of men built differently from him who enjoyed inflicting misery and degradation on a helpless and enslaved people. By contrast, Golema Mmidi seemed a dream he had evoked out of his own consciousness to help him live, to help make life tolerable. But if it was a dream, it was a merciful one, where women walked around all day with their bare feet and there were no notices up saying black men could not listen to the twitter and chatter of birds. The small brown speckled-breasted birds who lived in such huge colonies in Botswana were fat, gorged things. Dinorego solved the mystery, for him, of their eating habits. He took Makhaya a little way into the bush and broke open the surface of the earth. It crawled, just under the surface, with the soft juicy bodies of white ants, and thousands of birds lived on these juicy morsels the day long.

So many of the barefoot women, too, competed to do him a little favour. He never had to worry about where a cup of tea, which smelled like wood smoke, would come from, or what he would eat for the next meal. It was always there, brought by a rush of eager hands. Paulina Sebeso had to stand back and watch this jealously, but no other woman felt jealous as he shared out his attention among them all equally and then stood up at the end of the day and went his own way. Dinorego was very impressed by Makhaya's relationship with the women. It seemed to him that Makhaya was well versed in ancient African customs where the man maintained his dignity and self-control in front of women, except that in former times this man had maintained it over a harem of concubines, while Makhaya had none.

Mma-Millipede, of course, shared every secret with her friend Dinorego, and since Paulina Sebeso was like their own flesh and blood, being also a northerner, they were both anxious that she obtain for herself this young man whom they both loved. Nor could Dinorego fail to notice how Paulina trailed silently behind them each evening on their homeward journey and that every recognition of her existence by Makhaya filled her big black eyes with the shining look of rain falling on wet leaves. Not that Makhaya failed to notice it either, after some time. His first reaction was one of helpless surprise, because, in spite of his good looks, he was quite unaccustomed to being adored by a woman in a single-minded way. That is, adoration was patient and waiting while love or, if you liked, plain sexual passion banged everything about. It either shouted or thought it knew too much, and it had always left him cold and had not involved his heart. Therefore, if he wanted to get involved now it would be on his own terms and at his own pace. He ignored Paulina Sebeso as carefully as he ignored all the women, but he also sat in her yard and drank wood smoke tea until the stars came out. Then he would stand up and say, abruptly, "Well, I'll be going now."

But Paulina Sebeso had a very pretty little girl who walked like a wind-blown leaf, and Makhaya was in a mood just then to like a little girl like that. He turned up one Saturday afternoon with a box in which he had thin strips of rubber, packing straw, glue, and green paint, and together he and the child set out to make grass for her miniature village. They worked the whole afternoon on this in absorbed silence, like two children of the same age who took life very seriously. Paulina worked nearby in silence too. Like all the other women who were now working daily on the sheds and dams, she had to stamp large quantities of sorghum for a week's supply of porridge. Now, all over the village the sound could be heard of wooden pestles being pounded into wooden stamping blocks. Every three minutes or so Paulina paused and poured a minute quantity of water into the stamping block to soften the hard orange and pink corn seeds. This in turn made the crushed, powdery corn quite damp, and once she had winnowed away the husks, she had to spread out the corn meal on sacks to dry. She was so preoccupied that it was some time before she noticed Makhaya standing nearby, observing her. It upset the accuracy with which she hurled the pestle into the stamping block, and she looked up at him in exasperation, wanting him to go away.

"I want some tea," he said by way of explanation. "But I'll light the fire and make it."

"Goodness!" she said in alarm, holding onto the thick wooden stick. "Don't touch the fire. It's a woman's work."

Makhaya narrowed his eyes, that amused magical smile on his face. "Goodness!" he said, imitating her speech. "It's time you learned that men live on this earth too. If I want to make tea, I'll make it, and if I want to sweep the floor, I'll sweep it."

Paulina shook her head and continued stamping.

Makhaya turned the world upside down every day. He issued orders no one could counter, and he issued them with a smile that begged for an excuse for being the sole controller of everyone's life and the stars and the moon too.

"Quiet men are dangerous," she said to herself with a smile.

But they filled the world with peace, these quiet men. Everything ran on smooth wheels with a mathematical order and precision. The child sat near her village, carefully painting the grass green while the man, with equal care, scraped out the old ash with a flat stick and set a fresh, crumpled paper on the outdoor fireplace. Paulina watched the fire-making with a critical eye, and it occurred to her for the first time why the ancestors had set certain jobs aside for women and certain jobs for men. Men and women were unalike mentally. Look at how this man built a fire! He treated each stick as a separate living entity, and because of his respect for each stick, he moved his hands slowly, with many pauses, placing the firewood down at carefully calculated angles. This fire was set for a limited purpose. It was meant to boil water for tea and burn beautifully, without smoke, in a straight blue flame. A woman worked differently. She grasped a bunch of sticks in her hand, but it wasn't the fire only but a thousand other purposes that fire would serve. At one moment it had to burn brightly but the next the flames had to be pulled apart and simmer the pot of meat. A fire was only a rag bag to a woman, and because of this she threw the firewood on the flames in haphazard confusion. In protest, the fire smoked like mad and food and tea and wood smoke all got mixed up together. But would people ever eat and stay alive if housework was so precise and calculated like this bright, smokeless, quick-burning fire?

From habit, she dropped the wooden pestle and rushed towards one of the huts. She would catch the last of the flames and mess them up with a clutter of wood and set the porridge pot over this smoke haze for the evening meal. Jarred by this sudden, frantic activity, the mathematical fire-maker and tea-maker retreated with a profound look of annoyance on his face. He could not even bear to look at the way Paulina sloshed the tea into the teacups. He walked towards the thornbush hedge and stood with his hands in his pockets, looking towards the horizon.

But the look of annoyance was soon banished because the sun was about to drop down behind the flat horizon. It was just a big yellow ball and the air danced with sparkling crystals. The faint blue mists shivered like homeless dogs and slyly crept into the hedged yard for a bit of warmth.

"Here's your tea, my friend," the woman said, approaching him.

"Thank you," Makhaya said, politely, ever careful to keep himself the homeless foreign alien.

"You must not say 'thank you' once you are used to a person," the woman said.

"It depends on whether the person is used to me," he said. "Are you?"

She looked at him, half-laughing, half-puzzled. He always confused her with the speed with which he replied to careless, thoughtless remarks and the way he had of taking conversations up and down hills and valleys and mountains.

"I should be afraid to say I am used to a person like you," she said.

The answer pleased him and he turned again to the sunset. He wanted no one to be as rash as to say they understood his soul, especially when he had put up so many "no trespass" signs. He wanted everyone as the background to his thoughts, not through arrogance, but that this emotional detachment was essential to real love and respect. The distances also revealed to him his true relationship to both friend and foe, and in the end both friends and foes might be acceptable if they always lived on the other side of the hill. But within all this, as Mma-Millipede had discovered, he employed a number of undercover tricks to bring him close enough to those whose warmth and love he craved. Ah, but happiness, anyway, was dirt cheap in Botswana. It was standing still, almost in the middle of nowhere, and having your face coloured up gold by the setting sun. He heard the small girl approach behind him and sit down next to her mother to sip tea. He had found out from her that she also had a brother, a few years older than she was.

Without turning around he asked, "Where's the boy?"

"He's at the cattle post, looking after the cattle," Paulina said.

"You ought to employ someone older who does not need an education," he said.

She kept quiet. Wages were a problem. An employed person had to be paid a monthly salary, and she barely earned thirty pounds a year from the sale of her cattle. Cattle were all that stood between her children and herself and outright starvation, and she had to keep the costs down. Makhaya turned round and looked at her. He was only thinking about the small boy. If an old man like Dinorego had found the cattle business such a harsh life, how much more terrible must it be for a young boy. Paulina looked down.

"I know the child must attend school," she said. "But I cannot afford to employ somebody."

"How many cattle do you have?" he asked.

"Eighty," she said.

He was silent a moment, making a swift mental

calculation. "You must sell the damn beasts," he said.

She looked up, shocked. A Motswana without any cattle at all might as well be dead. "I cannot do that," she said.

"But you will have nine hundred pounds in the bank," he said. "It's enough money to live on for four or five years, and the boy will be free to attend school."

The idea of selling all the cattle was totally unacceptable to her. She could not see beyond cattle to anything else which would offer her a haven of security. If her husband had been alive, the boy would most certainly be at school. She compressed her lips and looked at Makhaya with hard, realistic eyes.

"Why do you care?" she said roughly. "You are no relative of mine."

He laughed because he was unsure if her remark meant he was someone out to swindle her.

"We'll talk about relatives some other day," he said. "I'm now talking about those damn beasts who are more of a burden than a help to you. I've said, after you've sold the burden, you will know what you are eating for four or five years. That's time enough to look around and find another way of earning a living. I'll help you because I'm interested in the same thing."

She was unconvinced. "Why do you want to help me?" she asked. "Why don't you go and get rich by yourself. Each man helps himself in this world."

He looked at her exasperated. "I'm not really necessary to anyone, least of all to Gilbert," he said. "I can feel myself leaving this country, perhaps even tomorrow. But if you think you need my help, I'll stay and help you."

"Perhaps you had better go away," she said in a shaken voice.

She could not follow the strange twists and turns of his mind, and this filled her with a bitter, furious despair. No one could accept anything they could not understand. Besides, when had anyone helped another, free of charge? It wasn't a custom. She looked up at him apprehensively. If he really believed her and went away, she would die. He returned her look with a look of speculative calculation. There were other ways of saying what he had to say, but he was forcing friendship and understanding on her because he needed this in a woman more than he needed anything else. He walked across the short space that separated them and sat near her on the jutting mud foundation of the hut.

"You don't understand, Paulie," he said. "Poor people are poor because they don't know how to get rich. I also live in this small dark room and I have counted the change over and over. Now, I'm tired of counting the change. I'm going to be a millionaire. But poverty is like glue. All poor people stick on me and they have to become millionaires with me. By this I mean that there will be no poverty left in Africa by the time I die."

He sat there in silence. There was much more he wanted to say. There was space enough in her country for the poor to become rich, and the evil that men do to each other was not to be found in such major proportions here. He could feel it and this was at the base of his new feeling of hope and peace. She sat in silence too, while her mind worked in that one-track feminine way. There was a point at which love reached the over-limit stage and then levelled itself out into a still plateau. It was like a nightmare and it was lonely. Yet he kept on adding and adding to the nightmare with his gentle, persuasive speeches.

"Tell me how you will help me to get rich," she said at last.

Makhaya looked at her in surprise. Millionaire-hood was not a practical reality to him but a strange subconscious process. There would be a day when he would hold out his hand and all the money in the world would fall into it. This he was sure of because his whole life was strained to that point, and he simply left it to his subconscious to do the building, brick by brick. One day, the whole superstructure would be there, glittering with gold walls. Why, he had spent a lifetime absorbing all the tenderness, sorrow, and fear of the world, and there was a web and design in it. He smiled at her.

"I don't know," he said. "Except that sometimes I think I am God. I don't see why God, who owns the whole earth and heaven, should starve. He'll use his brains, won't he?"

Paulina hid her face in her hands and laughed. But the next moment she sat up with a jolt. The fire was slowly dying away with no one to attend to it. She jumped up and rushed over with outstretched hands to catch the last, flickering flames and thrust them back vigorously into life again. The thick porridge was done. There was only the goat meat to boil in the weak curry-powder gravy.

She looked over her shoulder at Makhaya mischievously and said, "Will you eat food in my house, God?"

Chapter 10

Matenge came back to Golema Mmidi in mid-August and found himself faced with the progress of mankind. Commoners were up and about everywhere, busy like ants, building dams for themselves. They were also laughing and had some new language up their sleeve, like "cash-crops". This sent Matenge into a fuming rage. Barely ten years ago the commoner had always to approach a chief or sub-chief and ask him for permission to progress. This desire for progress had usually taken the form of wanting to build a small brick house with a tin roof. But brick houses were for chiefs alone, and how could an ordinary commoner want to bring himself up to the level of a chief? Or again, he might desire to set up a borehole for watering his cattle. The chief could say yes or no. If in some demented mood he said yes and then the commoner prospered, it would not be for long. This unfortunate man would one day be notified by the chief that a road was to be built in the pathway of his borehole. Would the commoner please quit? And not so many months after that the chief acquired a new watering place for his cattle.

Although he did not know it, Matenge was a thoroughly cornered rat, partly because his brother was playing football with him, and partly because he was faced with an entirely new situation in Golema Mmidi. There were too many independent-minded people there, and tragedies of life had liberated them from the environmental control of the tribe. Never before had people been allowed to settle permanently on the land as they were doing in Golema Mmidi. In the not so very far back bad old days, those who desired to be permanent farmers had had their huts burned down and been driven back to the villages. So the cheerful Paramount Chief Sekoto, who casually broke the rules and needed to possess no man's soul, was perhaps an unconscious assistant of the progress of mankind. But all things are unpredictable under the social structure of African tribalism. It seems to hold within itself terrible and secret currents which are geared toward eternal enmity of the individuals who stand alone; and who knew if one day Chief Sekoto might not turn demented too and unleash a bombshell of destruction on Golema Mmidi.

Matenge's crises were always silently prepared. No one ever knew what was going on in that lonely mountain-top which was his soul. The village was just presented with his thunderstorms, and their fierceness and savage intensity were the outcome of months of brooding. But he was ailing these days and it took him longer than usual to find his new victim. His dizzy spells alarmed him and he spent many hours quietly relaxing on his porch in his royal purple dressing gown, while he kept his servants dancing up and down in attendance on his needs. Being only servants and anxious to please him, they also kept him informed of all the developments in the village. The name of Paulina Sebeso was frequently mentioned by the servants.

Yet, at this time, a far greater crisis than any Matenge could ever produce was to strike down on the village of Golema Mmidi and the country as a whole. It all began so quietly. The weather was the usual for this time of the year; that is, from mid-August to mid-September the country was suddenly and abruptly plunged into the most intense and stifling heat. Scorching winds, too, blew in from the west, bringing with them huge swirling columns of red desert dust. All this misery was welcomed. The intense heat precipitated the first summer downpour. The old people and cattlemen knew this, and they remained contented in the swirling dust and heat. They never had any calendars but when they looked towards the sky, they knew it was September, the month when the rain clouds gathered. No matter that this was a country of two years of good rain and seven years of drought, the rain clouds always gathered in September.

But September came around and no rain clouds gathered in the sky. At the cattle posts, far out in the bush, the spade-dug wells were drying up, but still the cattlemen were not unduly worried. The huge, hulking, cavernous-bodied, russet brown Tswana cow was a strange beast. No one seems to know of its origin, but everyone knew of its adaptation to the hazards of local climatic conditions and of its ability to go for long periods without food or water. Man and beast had always lived this way. If there was no food or water for a man, then there was none for his cattle either. Both were as close to each other as breathing, and it had never been regarded as strange that a man and his cattle lived the same life. No doubt the cattlemen who lived in the lonely, isolated cattle posts at first stared in disbelief when their cattle began dropping dead before their very eyes. There were always droughts. There had been many in each man's lifetime, but never in the memory of man had the cattle dropped dead. By the time the men panicked, hundreds and thousands of cattle had died.

The truth was no one knew what to do, and the authorities, who by this time were becoming aware of the extent of the tragedy that was taking place in the bush, had no way of establishing communication with the thousands of men at the isolated, unmapped cattle stations. Eventually, all the cattlemen were to be driven out of the bush, overcome by thirst, each trailing behind a few emaciated beasts. But they were a reasoning steady crowd, these cattlemen. They moved slowly and thought slowly, often with a quiet humour. It was reasonable to them that the vultures should gather above a man's cattle post, for who could bury all these cattle which were dying daily? They watched in calm apprehension as one beast after another toppled dead to the ground. This was reasonable too. When had the dry season ever spanned ten long months? The rain of the previous year had all fallen in November. There had been a day in November when the sky had emptied itself in one long angry downpour. Then all the rain had fled away. But the lack of rain had not troubled the cattlemen. They had their wells along silted-up river beds where the water flowed underground all year round. True enough, the grazing had been burned bone dry by the hot January sun, but they had an ancient belief that bone dry grazing was better for their cattle than fresh, green grass, wet with dew. Now, nodding their heads they slowly absorbed a new truth: if cattle ate bone dry grass for ten months, a day would arrive when all cattle would drop down dead.

Once they reached this point in their reasoning, all the cattlemen picked up their long sticks and began driving what was left of their herds back to the villages to arrive there with ghastly tales of how the bush was one big graveyard. But the vultures are feasting, they added humorously.

The first wave of cattlemen who had exhausted their reasoning powers arrived in the village of Golema Mmidi in the late afternoon. They hastily erected kraals for their cattle with thornbush and instructed their wives to water the cattle sparingly. Then they retired to the yard of one of their fellows, and all sat in a circle on wooden stools, silently drinking bowls of sour milk porridge. Disaster had indeed struck down swiftly on their small world, and each man sat in a mountain of aloof reserve to prevent his fellow from starting the sorrowful tale:

"My friend, I had two hundred cattle just yesterday. Out of this, one hundred and twenty have died. I have just counted the beasts. I now have eighty."

They had seen the bush strewn with dead cattle on their way home. No one had stopped to look behind at the weak cows who had lain down to calve and die in the process of giving birth. The one thought in each man's mind had been to hasten home, even if he only had one beast left. Cattlemen could talk about this with humour and resignation to any other person but one of their fellows. It was not long before this group of silent men was joined by that super reasoner, Dinorego. He came into the yard with his cheerful shuffle, holding on to the remnants of his tattered coat. The men moved aside immediately. They respected and trusted no one more deeply than Dinorego. Once the old man had seated himself, the owner of the yard, a tall, taciturn man named Rankoane, threw the stiff, dried-up carcass of a small wild buck into the circle of men.

"Look what I found, my friend," Rankoane said. "It's not only the cattle which are dying."

The big dark eyes of the little animal were wide open, and he lay on his side with his four delicate legs stretched out stiffly, just the way the cattle lay when they dropped down dead. The men stared at it in fascination, really seeing death for the first time—they could not bear to look on their cattle in this posture of death. Rankoane enjoyed this effect. He enjoyed the contemplation of death and was one of the few men who could stare at it boldly. He bent down and removed the carcass and threw it to one side. Dinorego nodded his head several times, profoundly.

"We have received this news some days ago," he

said. "The news came by phone to my son, Gilbert. It was the police officer, George Appleby-Smith, who phoned. He said, 'Gilbert, do you know of the way cattle and wild beasts are dying in the bush?' And Gilbert said, 'I am not surprised. Look at how it rained last year, all on one day in November.' I was present when this phone call came, and my son Gilbert put down the phone, struck with pity. My heart too was struck with pity. I said, 'The Good Lord has prevented me from keeping something which dies.'"

The men looked at Dinorego with deep interest. The mention of the name of Gilbert had suddenly filled their hearts with hope, where before had been a passive resignation. No one had any clear idea of why he had headed home except that it seemed the most reasonable thing to do. But they were all members of the cattle co-operative and greatly prided themselves on having joined this new and strange association. Perhaps Gilbert, who had new ideas each day, would tell them what to do with all the cattle they could no longer feed.

"What has Gilbert to say about the deaths?" one of the men prompted tentatively.

Dinorego looked at the men triumphantly. "The rain has not come." he said. "But still we will plough. Come, let us go and see Gilbert."

With one abrupt gesture, the men put down their porridge bowls and stood up. Rankoane's wife, who was watering the cattle nearby, looked at them in amazement. They looked like men about to go into battle, so stern and concentrated were their expressions. Just as they were about to leave the yard, Paulina Sebeso approached them. She clasped her hands politely together in greeting but she was wild with anxiety. She fixed her eyes on Rankoane.

"Please spare a moment, Rra Rankoane," she said.

"I want to ask you something."

Rankoane detached himself from the group and walked towards her with his angry-looking expression. Rankoane was always rude and offhand to women.

"What is it?" he asked impatiently.

"Your cattle post is near mine," Paulina said. "Why didn't you persuade my son to come home with you? What's the good of him staying in the bush when there is no water and the cattle are dying?"

A queer, guarded look crept into Rankoane's eyes. "So, your son has not come home, Paulina Sebeso?" he asked quietly.

"I don't understand you, Rankoane," she said, wildly. "What are you saying?"

The man shrugged. He had more than enough troubles to bear. His whole livelihood had almost vanished before his very eyes.

"I told your son to go home two weeks ago," he said. "I expected him to be here, that's why I did not stop at your cattle post today."

He walked away to join the group of men, but then he turned round once and looked back at Paulina with a twisted expression of pain on his face. At the same time he was trying to escape responsibility by not telling the woman why he had ordered her son home two weeks previously. It must have been just about this time too, after he had brought the cattle back to the kraal for the night, that Paulina's son had come to him.

"I don't know what's wrong with me, Uncle," the boy had said. "I am coughing up blood every day."

But Rankoane knew at one glance what was wrong. Tuberculosis was the one major killer in the country, and the small boy with his red feverish eyes was seriously ill with it. Also, the diet they were eating now, plain porridge with salt and water and no milk, must have brought the boy's ailment to a serious stage. Rankoane merely smiled because he did not want to alarm the boy who looked like a thin, bony scarecrow in his father's oversized jacket.

"We are all coughing," he said. "The reason why? There is too much dust and no rain to settle it. Dust in the lungs causes one to cough up blood. The one way to cure it is by drinking beer, but since you are young and cannot drink the beer you must go home tomorrow with the cattle and your mother will take you to hospital."

The small boy grinned at him cheerfully, with big, white teeth. He was amused at Rankoane's reference to beer and the man-to-man tone of his voice. Still, he was worried. He could not take the cattle back to the village and burden his mother with them.

"Can't I leave the cattle in your care until I come back from the hospital, Uncle?" he asked.

Rankoane had shifted uncomfortably. He was now drawing up a half bucket of water from his well and he could not add to his own worries. Besides, Paulina Sebeso was a resourceful woman and she would know what to do. He explained this to the boy who nodded. The last thing he would get from his mother was a scolding. She made a joke of life and he already knew what she would say when he unexpectedly arrived home: "Goodness, Isaac, don't tell me you have eaten up all your rations." And he would say: "No, Mama, I have come home because I am coughing up blood every day." This would most surely strike his mother as unusual, as she would not know of Rankoane's story about the dust in the lungs. The thought of his mother and her surprise and concern filled the small boy's heart with warm comfort. He stood up and walked back happily to his own roughly built hut, and it was the memory of this last conversation he had had with the boy that made Rankoane look back at

Paulina Sebeso with a pained expression. He ought not to have done so, for his look froze Paulina to the ground and she could not move, so lifeless and numb was the feeling in her arms and legs. Several times Rankoane's wife called to her, after the men had walked away. Eventually, she put the bucket down and walked over to Paulina.

"I say, my friend, what's the matter?" asked Rankoane's wife.

Paulina looked at Rankoane's wife almost bitterly. Women who had husbands made the deep well of her own loneliness more acute to her.

"I'm thinking of going to the cattle post tomorrow to fetch my son," she said.

"My, but you are brave, Paulina Sebeso," the other woman said. "I hear that the bush is now full of dangerous beasts who are feasting off the dead cattle."

Paulina Sebeso stared at Rankoane's wife. People in comfort and safety said things like this to people who always faced the storms and winters of life.

"You're a silly fool, Segametse," she said and walked away with her head held up proudly. But halfway to her own home she almost dropped it to the ground in despair, and so hangdog and depressed was she that she nearly collided into Makhaya, who stood at the entrance of her yard, looking out towards the smeared, murky red glow which was the sunset.

"Oh Makhaya," she said, looking up at him with a taut, strained face. "My whole life is turned upside down."

"It's nothing," he said, smiling down at her. "The boy is young. It wouldn't occur to him to come home with the cattle. We'll go together to the cattle post tomorrow and bring him and the cattle back to the village."

And that was all he said before walking away, back

to the farm. There was nothing else he offered her except his kindness and help. On other days she questioned this relentlessly because he kept it unrelated to any human feeling. He seemed to ignore the fact that he awakened a fire in someone else's life with his generosity. But on this day it lifted the weight off her arms and legs. He had not even asked her, as Rankoane had done, if her son had come home but had simply produced immediate solutions to her trouble. This filled her eyes with a quiet, wondering look. Yet Makhaya could have ended this odd game with a gesture or a few words or even a look. He knew how much Paulina Sebeso loved him, but still he hesitated. He would not have liked it if Paulina gave up and stopped loving him because it was like a warm sun on all the shadows of his life. It was just that there were things he could not put in words, that a woman's life was a clutter of small everyday things—of babies, gossip, pots, food, fires, cups, and plates—and that all these things had crashed into his consciousness during the month he had worked on the dams and tobacco sheds with the women.

Makhaya walked into the farm yard just as the cattlemen were rising from their discussion with Gilbert. They looked at Makhaya curiously with his strange, strongly marked facial bone structure. They had yet to learn from their wives about the tobacco project and the dams that were being built to trap some of the storm water, but on this evening there was no time for introduction to the stranger. The sight and sound of their cattle crashing dead on the ground were still full in the men's eyes, and they walked away with the heavy tread of people who were grieved beyond consolation. Makhaya turned and looked at his friend Gilbert and started in surprise. He knew Gilbert so well by now that he could judge his every mood, and on this evening he was in a mood of high elation, even though he kept his face quite serious and listened attentively to Dinorego, who was summing up the situation for him.

Dinorego was saying, "We can progress too, even though we are uneducated men. The mind of an uneducated man works like this: he is a listener and a believer. Most of all he is a believer. The uneducated man has been condemned for many years by the authorities. They came to us and said, 'We have found new grazing land in the west. Move the cattle over because the eastern side has no more grazing left.' Yet no one moved. The west is lion country. Some time ago people were eaten by lions and that is enough. This is a belief in our minds that we will be eaten by lions therefore we cannot go west. Today, once all the cattle have died, the authorities will say, 'You see, we told you.' But it is strange to me that they did not create the belief that the uneducated man could shoot the lions."

He paused and looked at the two men with his shrewd, twinkling eyes and both men burst out laughing. It was only a pity that Dinorego was not the Prime Minister of Botswana, as no one could defeat his reasoning power or his faith in progress. He also liked an audience and spread out his hands appreciatively and continued:

"Nearly every agriculture man knows about the progress of the uneducated man. They are always coming to us saying, 'Look, I can show you how to plough eighty morgan of sorghum.' Once he has produced the field of eighty morgan, the uneducated man will be consumed by jealousy and try to do the same. What he sees, he believes. But he never questions a matter like an educated man. The miracle must be placed before his eyes, then he will try to perform a miracle too."

Gilbert looked at the old man intently, the blue

flame of elation dancing brightly in his eyes. "What would you say if I said that the deaths of all these cattle, in Golema Mmidi, are a miracle? What would you say if I said I was hoping it would happen?" he asked.

The old man kept deadly silent as he suspected a trap in these unexpected words of Gilbert, and Makhaya leaned forward with interest as he was now about to hear the reason for the suppressed excitement of his friend. Gilbert raised his hands like a gambler who foresees only the gains that will come without any losses. He had three years of research and experiments behind him, but the cattle population of Golema Mmidi had been too huge and unwieldly for his plans. For planned and scientific production of high-grade beef, he needed a drastically reduced herd. He also needed the men near the food growing areas where beef production and food production could be combined. He had everything on hand too, the latest developments in fodder crops for cattle feed and silage making and his own experiments with the natural grasses of Botswana and imported grass seed.

To the cattlemen he had merely presented the government's emergency plans for dealing with the situation, and these were that there was to be an accelerated slaughter of emaciated beasts at the abattoir. These emaciated beasts would be boiled down into corned beef. This slaughter of cattle would bring in about ten pounds per cow for each man, which was better than nothing at all, and it was designed to relieve the situation until free emergency rations would arrive in about one month's time. Thus each man would contribute so many head of cattle from his herd, and those that were left would be kept alive for one month on the fodder in the farm's silage pits. The men had agreed to this arrangement. They had also agreed to retain within the co-operative a certain sum of the money they received for the wholesale slaughter of cattle. This would act as an incentive to the cattlemen to recoup from their losses and restock their herds. He also told the men that since they had an organized cattle co-operative in the village the government had already agreed to drill a free borehole, whose equipment and management would in future be taken over by the co-operative.

This was all he had told them, but to Makhaya and Dinorego, on whom he depended for the fulfilment of his dreams, he allowed his mind to leap ahead to three years from that date when all the thick forests of thornbush that surrounded Golema Mmidi had given way to acres and acres of cultivated fields on which crops grew, under irrigation, the year round. Golema Mmidi would have about ten to twelve boreholes and reservoirs by that time and as many more big dams to hold back every drop of storm water. And he willed his two companions to see it, how Golema Mmidi would supply the whole country with the fresh fruit and vegetables it lacked, and apart from bringing in the highest profits for the best grade beef, it would also create the first industries in the country. Why, he had already picked up a cigarette manufacturer and made him sign a contract to buy tobacco grown by the Golema Mmidi tobacco growing co-operative, and this manufacturer was already building a factory in northern Botswana.

"People have said to me, 'Oh, forget farming in this dry country,'" he said intensely. "I've kept my mouth shut all these years, but my eyes have taught me that Botswana is a farmer's heaven. It's better than countries with a high rainfall. Farming under irrigation is controlled and predictable farming. Also, the long dry season is more suited to crops like potatoes and tobacco, which need well-drained soil. We've a minimum of crop destroying pests to deal with too, and the soil is rich and fertile."

He looked at Makhaya with his eyes full of dreams, because Makhaya had proved himself the magician who could make tobacco co-operatives appear overnight. He wanted Golema Mmidi to be co-operative in everything as that was the only way of defeating the land tenure system in the tribal reserves and the only way of defeating subsistence agriculture which was geared to keeping the poor man poor until eternity. Makhaya smiled back quietly and affectionately at his friend. He liked this kind of talk. He liked the idea that the whole of Golema Mmidi would be full of future millionaires. It blended in with his own dreams about Africa because he could not see it other than as a continent of future millionaires, which would compensate for all the centuries of browbeating, hatred, humiliation, and worldwide derision that had been directed to the person of the African man. And communal systems of development which imposed co-operation and sharing of wealth were much better than the dog-eat-dog policies, take-over bids, and grab-what-you-can of big finance. Therefore, in Makhaya's mind, the poverty and tribalism of Africa were a blessing if people could develop sharing everything with each other.

"I like everything you say, Gilbert," he said with deep feeling. They looked at the old man, who always had the last word on everything. But Dinorego kept silent. He was regretting that the world had decided to improve itself only when he had become such an old man with a few years left to live. Now, each time he decided he would rest in peace, he kept on learning more about life, and he was not feeling so contented about dying.

"I'm going to the cattle post tomorrow," Makhaya said, breaking the silence.

Gilbert and the old man looked at him in surprise.

These were the familiar words of a Batswana man, but they sounded strange on Makhaya's lips.

Makhaya wanted to laugh out loud at their surprise. He felt no desire whatsoever to own these huge beasts. They would be an intolerable encumbrance to him. Hesitantly, he explained that he had promised Paulina he would accompany her to her cattle post to see if everything was all right with her son.

"The boy may be ill," he said. "She expected him to come home with someone named Rankoane whose cattle post is near hers, but he says the boy should have arrived home two weeks ago. Rankoane says the wells have dried up."

It chilled Gilbert to hear this and he felt a sharp stab of pain at the way he had light-heartedly talked of scientific beef production amidst all this tragedy.

"Mack, you know it's a whole day's walk to the cattle posts," he said. "The three of us will leave first thing in the morning with the Land-Rover. I also want to see for myself what is happening in the bush."

He looked across at Makhaya with all the elation gone out of his eyes. His mind had jumped too far ahead into the future, but the present was painful and terrible.

"I hope the boy is only ill," he said. "He may be dead."

Makhaya said nothing, yet once Maria came out of the hut and called the three men to eat, his stomach was just tight, painful knots and he excused himself and walked away to his hut. He lay down for some time in his hut, in the darkness, with a strange sensation of having no thoughts in his head, only to discover, with an explosive shock, that he had been talking to himself all the time. He had no idea of what he had been saying to himself because it was an incoherent expression of the concentration of pain inside him. What sort of man was he who only gave way to love under extreme pressure and pain? Perhaps, he had read somewhere, men and women just loved each other without reason or purpose, but he did not belong to this world, not when everything inside him was in revolt. If he loved Paulina now and admitted it to himself, it was because he sensed that she might be facing tragedy, and that she could not face it alone. He swung his legs off the bed, stood up, and walked out of the dark farm to the home of Paulina Sebeso. There was complete darkness in her yard as she was already in bed. He knocked on the door of the hut she used as a bedroom.

"Who is it?" she asked, as she was not yet asleep.

"Makhaya," he said, quietly.

She was silent awhile, then jumped out of bed and unlocked the door. He could not even see her face in this pitch dark night, and there was still this struggle within his aloof self, so uncertain was he of life.

"Gilbert will also be coming to the cattle post tomorrow," he said, oddly, excusing himself because he was about to invade her life through his fear of tomorrow.

She still kept silent, half-wanting to laugh and half-wanting to cry. Then she closed her eyes to add to the darkness, because nothing that you said seemed quite so bad when everything was dark.

"Makhaya," she said softly. "You mustn't think I'm a cheap woman, but I love you."

"Why cheap?" he said, amused. "There are no cheap women. Even those you buy love you, while we men rarely do. Perhaps I'll find out what love is like as we go along together."

Makhaya was thankful, too, for the dark as he entered her hut. For so long there was this grey graveyard in which he had lived. And who could tell what ghosts really do when they come alive in the dark night?

Chapter 11

It was just as though everything was about to die. The small brown birds had deserted the bush, and the bush itself no longer supplied the coverage and protection for the secret activities of the scarlet and golden birds. Here and there, faint patches of green clung to the topmost branches of tall thorn trees, but not a green thing survived near the sun-baked earth. The sky had lost that dense blue look of the winter days and spread itself out into a whitish film, through which the sun poured out molten heat in pulsating waves from dawn to dusk. In this desolation the vultures reigned supreme. They gathered on the ground in huge flocks of sixty to a hundred and held important discussions in hoarse, rough voices and flapped their long, sloppy brown feathers in imperious indignation. They could afford to be imperious, indignant and important, for they were to be a burial society for over six hundred thousand cattle. They were amazed and wondering if they would manage it all or if they should send messages to fellow brethren in Africa and India. But whatever their deliberations, they were fearless and proud, for these mean, fierce birds knew that they were always the last visitors on a stricken part of the earth.

Barely three miles away from the village of Golema Mmidi the impact of all this struck the small party that had left for the cattle post early in the morning. During the night, a cow that had belonged to one of the cattlemen had lain down to calve and died in the process. A jackal had hovered near her the whole night and at dawn set himself to devour the newborn calf. The approach of the Land-Rover disturbed him and he arose and slunk away into the bush. Gilbert slowed down the vehicle near the cow and his exclamation—"Oh, this is terrible!"—hardly conveyed the deep sense of shock Makhaya felt. From that day Makhaya was to become peculiarly Motswana in his outlook. Coming from a country of green hills and fresh bubbling streams, he was from that day to treasure every green shoot that sprang up in this dry place, and he would fear to waste even a drop of water. Paulina was the only one who was not deeply perturbed by what she saw. She had lived through times like this before, when the bush was bare and the ploughing season delayed indefinitely. To her, it even seemed like an unreal and lovely spring morning when life was just beginning anew again instead of dying, and her feelings relived over and over again a whole night's dream.

He just sat there beside her looking as cool and aloof and unchanged as yesterday, while nothing of her own life was left to her, as though she had become an appendage of his body like an arm or a leg. It wasn't a pleasant feeling as no secure promises had been made. On the other hand, a woman distrusted extravagant promises and, on the other, lived in fear of the silence of a reserved man who only expressed himself in deeds. Maybe women invented marriage, as their imaginations had invented most other things in man's social life. They can't help saying, "Are you my property? I must own you." And now Paulina busied her mind with these things while the sky and the bush exploded into a hot, white glare of heat.

Gilbert turned round and half-smiled at all the dreams in the woman's eyes.

"Am I still going in the right direction, Paul?" he asked. "The bush is so changed, I can't make out a thing."

That is, if he ever had. Like the Tswana language,

the bush belonged to all the Batswana people, who had created its footpaths and mapped out its length and breadth in their minds. It had often amazed him to discover that cattlemen drove their cattle home, through the bush, in pitch darkness, with an unerring sense of direction, while he, Gilbert, had several times lost his direction within the fenced farm lands, and his legs and arms bore lots of scars from having pitched himself into a barbed-wire fence at night. But Paulina had footed it this way every three or four months to take her son his food rations and see if all was well with him at the cattle post, and not so long ago, the call of birds had filled these empty spaces. They were always after something, these lovely birds, and she had always kept corn seed in the pocket of her skirt to scatter along the pathway. Now, the vultures, full and gorged, adorned the bare trees, and beneath their resting places lay the white, picked bones of the dead cattle. Those in the trees stared arrogantly at the passing vehicle, and those on the ground merely waddled out of the way. They were the kings of the bush and would remain so throughout this long year of no rain and no crops.

They passed a few empty drinking pools in the bush, and around these were scattered the carcasses of the tiny wild buck. Hundreds had gathered at their favourite drinking places, because about this time every year storm clouds brooded on the horizon and the rain fell down in blinding sheets of water and the scene changed overnight into carpets of fine green grass and splashes of purple and yellow flowers and the drinking pools filled up with sky blue water. The memory of all this drove them to their drinking pools, where they died. The cattlemen had a similar memory. Towards the end of the long dry season they too left their watering places along the river beds, and moved with their cattle into the bush where the grass grew in tangled confusion under the trees, and watered their cattle in the drinking pools of the wild buck. A few of the cattlemen, expecting rain at any time, had deviated towards these water pools on the journey homeward, only to have their huge herds fall down there and die. It happened over and over in Botswana that year.

Long before they reached Paulina's cattle post they saw the vultures circling above it in the sky. This marked it out right away as one of the death points. Once they drew close, they could see that not a living thing moved on the ground. All those eighty cattle lay scattered about, quite still, quite dead. It was like the final statement of all the terrible story of the bush. But there was still hope in the heart of the mother. She somehow expected her son to creep out of the lone and solitary hut, and she knew already how she would comfort him and dismiss all this as being of no account. So no one moved once Gilbert had stopped the car some twenty yards from the hut, and each person sat silently absorbing the desolate scene until the vultures began swooping down in a straight column on the already decomposing carcasses. This jerked the woman into action and she scrambled out of the car and raced towards the hut. But Makhaya reached the door before her and pulled her back and looked at her briefly with an angry expression. What was inside there was only for him to see. He pushed open the door and looked in. There was only a heap of clean, white bones lying on the floor. They lay in a curled, cramped position with the bones of the hands curved inward. The white ants and maggots had vied with each other to clear all the flesh off the little boy. And Makhaya stood there so silent and still, absorbing this terrible sight, confused and angry that there was only this dead, unanswering silence in his heart, as though he had only expected to see such sights. Paulina touched him on the back, and he swung around sharply with an expression of hurt surprise on his face.

"The boy is dead," he said sharply. "Why do you want to go in?"

"I must see the body," she said, but with dry, taut lips. "I must see the body because it is our custom."

"You see," he said, in a deliberately harsh voice. "All these rotten customs are killing us. Can't you see I'm here to bear all your burdens? Come on."

And he walked towards the car, knowing she would meekly follow him. He stood nearby and waited until she had climbed in, then he turned, almost with relief, to Gilbert, who sat at the wheel of the car with an ashen face.

"Is the boy dead, too?" Gilbert asked.

"Yes," Makhaya said shortly, and he had no idea that the hurt expression was still on his face. It was like having a smudge there and not knowing you had it. As though, Gilbert thought, he wanted to feel for everyone and get the matter over with. A small light of friendship and understanding stirred in Gilbert's eyes, and sensing this Makhaya spoke so trustingly to him:

"We don't know what has caused the death of the child, my friend," he said. "So, we will have to call the police. Could you please take my wife home and notify the police at the same time? I'll remain behind."

These few simple words put new life into Gilbert. He nodded briefly and turned the car round, and he and Paulina drove back in the direction of Golema Mmidi. Makhaya was left alone with the vultures. Surrounded by tragedy and seated in the shade of a ramshackle mud hut in the Botswana bush, he began to see himself. In retrospect he seemed a small-minded man. All his life he had wanted some kind of Utopia, and he had rejected in his mind and heart a world full of ailments and faults. He had run and run away from it, but now the time had come when he could run and hide no longer and would have to turn round and face all that he had run away from. Loving one woman had brought him to this realization: that it was only people who could bring the real rewards of living, that it was only people who give love and happiness.

As though to confirm his new trend of thought, he stirred a foot and found it brushed against a bundle of something, carefully tied up. He opened the bundle and in it was a collection of wood carvings, done by the small boy to occupy himself during the lonely hours of cattle herding. Among the assortment he picked up a thick porridge spoon, one and a half feet in length. A great deal of effort had been put into the production of this spoon. The small boy had probably intended it to be a gift to his mother. He had decorated the long handle with the twisting pattern of a snake's scaly body, and almost every detail, right up to the venomous eyes, had been reproduced. The design was bold and vivid and he had burned it into the wood with a red-hot piece of iron. Makhaya looked at it for some time, struggling to capture a living image of a child he did not know. He hoped he and Paulina would never create a child who would be expected to carry burdens beyond his age.

All the other carvings concerned themselves with the animals the small boy had observed in his surroundings, wild bucks, tortoises, monkeys, and birds. The birds were carved into a majestic, charcoal boat, and a half a dozen of them sat tail to tail with their heads in the air, like kings. One carving in particular aroused Makhaya's curiosity. The piece of wood was not more than six inches in length, and half of the grain was a livid flesh colour and the other was snow white. Out of this the boy had carved a minute crocodile with the same attention to detail as the snake design. Where had the boy seen a crocodile?

There were none along the eastern border area where the cattle grazed. And the surrounding area was thornbush forest, and the tiny piece of wood was a foreigner to the area.

He bent to tie up the bundle and the slight clatter of wood against wood made him look up at a comical drama that was played out barely six inches away from him. A wild jackal had been swiftly approaching the graveyard of cattle, and thinking himself alone with the vultures, he had concentrated his whole mind on his forthcoming meal. The unexpected noise brought him to a dead halt, and his first reaction was one of abject fear.

Looking neither left nor right, he almost slunk into the ground and then, a moment later, lifted one right paw in pathetic, pitiful apology, at the same time baring his sharp, jagged teeth in a savage snarl. Since the snarl went unchallenged, the poor thing quickly recovered itself and swivelled its foxy face in Makhaya's direction. The sun was behind the jackal, but as he turned, its reflection shone in his beautiful amber eyes in honey-gold flashes. He had a soft, thick, honey-gold coat too, with a contrasting streak of silver and black fur down his back. He stood for a few seconds, eyeing Makhaya fearfully and then turned and bounded away into the bush. It occurred to Makhaya that a wild animal was more afraid of man than a man need be of it, and its one thought was to retreat as far from man as possible. It seemed to him that in essence most of his reactions had been like those of the jackal, from the day he had been born. For some time his mouth quivered with amusement at the strange antics of the wild animal. Maybe that panic-stricken beast had a jackal society where he felt sane and secure, but no human society was sane and normal. Yet he needed to come to terms with his society because he needed a woman and children.

He could not go on thinking of the heap of bones that lay inside the hut, because death was like trying to clutch the air, and you had to let it be and slowly let it pass aside, without fuss and indignity. Instead, you had to concentrate the mind on all that was still alive and treat it as the most precious treasure you had ever been given. Besides, he had felt all the pain he was capable of feeling the night before, and it had directed his actions along this new path. So, he sat there thinking about his new life with Paulina. Even ordinary things like cups, brooms, pots, and houses were a pleasure for him to contemplate, once he had become aware of their existence, as though all these things would anchor him firmly to the earth. They also strengthened his resolve to be a future millionaire, for many a future millionaire must have had a dead child in his life who had died from lack of proper food, and he must have had a one-room hut in which he could hardly move and breathe. He must have lain awake at night, craving a four-room house with a kitchen, bathroom and taps, and mentally clothed this house with ornaments, chairs and beds, and he must have said he would always spend five pounds but get ten pounds back as change. If a man didn't have dreams like this, in Africa, he would end up food for the vultures too.

These horrible creatures guzzled and guzzled, seeming to have bottomless appetites. The wind swept huge columns of sand up into the sky, which carried the odour of death with it and brought more vultures, in thick, black patrols. They swooped down with their big wings outstretched like supersonic jets. Some of the fully gorged birds made way for the newcomers, flying up into the thorn trees and adorning the bare branches in monstrous, silent, carved postures. Even the wind blew according to its own mad pattern. For hours tiny gusts flew in harassed circles around the thornbush until they all converged into a roaring turmoil of air and red dust which would race madly for a mile or so along the earth and then sweep up and disperse itself in the sky.

Makhaya stood up at last, sickened by the ceaseless clack, clack of the vultures' beaks. Away from the little hut and the vultures was the endless, dead vista of scorched earth and twisted dry thornbush. He leaned against a dead tree and closed his eyes, all his capacity for thought slowly seeping out of him. This bush on all sides was the most awful life imaginable, and it occurred to Makhaya that it must have been this unrelieved, heavy isolation which had driven the lively-minded Dinorego out of the cattle business. Yet thousands of people lived like this, like trees, in all the lonely wastes of Africa, cut off even from communication with their own selves. Was it any wonder that life stood still if a man became a tree? Therefore, he, Makhaya, could run so far in search of peace, but it was contact with other living beings that a man needed most. Maybe even Utopias were just trees. Maybe. Maybe he walked around in hopeless circles, but at least he was attempting to reach up to a life beyond the morass in which all black men lived. Most men were waiting for the politicians to sort out their private agonies.

At this point he ceased thinking altogether, and the sun passed its topmost peak in the sky and began sinking towards the horizon. At about three o'clock Gilbert returned with the police officer George Appleby-Smith and a doctor. Makhaya sat in the car drinking a little water and eating food which Gilbert had brought along, while the policeman and doctor made their reports. Gilbert also sat in the car but he kept silent, too. Eventually the doctor came out of the hut and walked towards the car.

"I'd say the poor little fellow died of malnutrition," he said.

He kept quiet a moment, screwed up his eyes, and looked away. The hospitals were full of children who died in the posture of the little boy in the hut, their knees cramped up to their chins, their bony fingers curled into their palms like steel claws. Most of those who survived would be mental defectives or cripples—while this little boy had mercifully died.

"The policeman wants to know if it's all right to bury the boy here," he added quietly.

Only Makhaya moved. "I'll accept responsibility for that," he said. He turned round and picked up a small can of petrol, jumped out of the car, and walked to the hut. George Appleby-Smith stood in the dark hut, staring at the little heap of bones, with an expressionless face. All these sights were supposed to be all in a day's work to him. But he stored these experiences away to give him the courage to run his area the way he thought it ought to be run, even to befriending "security risks" like Makhaya. All those authorities had kicked up such a dust about his allowing a "security risk" to settle in Golema Mmidi, but they never had occasion to come out into the bush to see how children died, while he, George, saw everything, every day. He turned towards Makhaya with one of those very rare smiles.

"Hullo, Makhaya," he said. "You settling down?"

"You still sticking your neck out for me?" Makhaya countered, also smiling.

Makhaya bent and poured a little petrol over the heap of bones, struck a match, and within a few seconds converted the pathetic sight into ashes. Then he scooped up the ashes into a small container which was lying in a corner of the hut. There was not a trace of the agony and fright in which the little boy must have died. Apart from the tin container, the small boy's bedding, a half a bag of ant-riddled sorghum meal, and a badly burned porridge pot, there was nothing else in the hut. They took with them only the tin container and the tied-up bundle outside the hut. It was long past sundown when they arrived in the village of Golema Mmidi. Even George Appleby-Smith had nothing to say. Droughts and dead children made him lose his sense of humour, and he got into his own car with the doctor and drove away. Maria walked quickly into the yard in her aloof, serious way. The whole village knew by now that Paulina's child had died and they were all in her yard, not talking but just sitting in heavy silent groups, like the trees. Makhaya suddenly could not bear this most exacting of all African customs, not just then, not with his emotional involvement with Paulina. He handed the tin container to Maria.

"Please take this to Paulie," he said. "Tell her I thought it best to burn what was left of the child."

Gilbert walked with his wife to the home of Paulina but Makhaya walked to his own hut, still clutching the tied-up bundle of wood carvings, and dropped on the bed in a deep and dreamless sleep. An hour later Maria knocked on the door. She had a tray with food and a cup of tea. There was silence inside the hut so she pushed the door open and walked in, setting the tray down on the table. She stood looking down with a slight smile at the sleeping man. Being an African man he ought to have known that nothing happened on the continent of Africa without all Africans getting to know of it. In some mysterious way, the news had travelled around the village of Golema Mmidi that Makhaya had spent the previous night at Paulina's home, even though Paulina had made no mention of it to anyone. God knows what they expected of the poor man, but it had added a twist of drama to an everyday event of mourning a death, which event everyone had to participate in. People were genuinely sorry for the bereaved Paulina, but they soon forgot it when only Maria and Gilbert turned up for the show with the remains of the dead child in a tin container. A lively titter of whispering started and Maria heard it all, silly things that would keep women twittering for days. If you can't face a crowd you must be a person who hates people, irrespective of a lifetime of individual deeds of kindness to individual people. That's why deviationists and independent-minded people were so few in Africa. But it wasn't because of the crowd that she awoke Makhaya. They had dispersed and gone their way by now. It was because of Paulina and the way she blamed herself for the death of her child in a quiet, final and despairing way without the usual tears or hysterics. She kept on looking at everyone with that haughty stare as much as to say, "Why don't you all go away." Only Mma-Millipede suspected that this quiet attitude meant that Paulina might try to kill herself, and she had confided this aside to Maria and said that she would remain behind, even for the whole night if necessary.

Maria bent and shook the sleeping man awake. "Have some food," she said in a kind and gentle voice because she was sorry, in her personal and private way, for everyone's suffering.

Since she hesitated, he turned to this twin soul of privacy and isolation and asked, "Do you know what I saw today, Maria?"

"No," she said curiously.

"Even the trees were dying, from the roots upward," he said. "Does everything die like this?"

"No," she said. "You may see no rivers on the ground but we keep the rivers inside us. That is why all good things and all good people are called rain. Sometimes we see the rain clouds gather even though not a cloud appears in the sky. It is all in our heart."

He nodded his head, fully grasping this in its deepest meaning. There was always something on this earth man was forced to love and worship by reason of its absence. People in cloudy, misty climates worshipped the sun, and people of semi-desert countries worshipped the rain.

"Paulina is blaming herself for the death of the child," she added softly, frightened at involving herself in the feelings of this sensitive man.

"I knew she would," he said, and paused in his eating and looked up at her. "I couldn't say anything about it with everyone there. Have they gone away?"

"Yes, but Mma-Millipede is still there."

He put the unfinished plate of food on the tray and stood up, waiting for her to pick up the tray and leave the hut. Then he blew out the candle and picked up the bundle of wood carvings.

"What a way for you to come home, little boy," he whispered, and stepped out into the dark night. The wind had died down and the stars shone down in the low, black sky with full, green lights. The stars were always there to accompany a man's lonely footsteps. They had been with him on the night he first arrived in Botswana, and they were like sprays of flowers between the narrow, grim streets of the slums in which he had grown up. They would be there too after he passed away, and they were all the conviction he had that some quiet and good creator controlled and owned the earth.

Mma-Millipede was saying much the same thing to Paulina. They sat out in the yard, near a bonfire of logs which the men of the village had lit, as a sign of death in the house. He stood for a moment outside the range of the firelight and listened to the murmur of Mma-Millipede's voice. Not only Jesus Christ had observed this but Mma-Millipede too—that this earth was not the final abode of man. It was a place of sorrows, a wilderness in which his soul wandered in restless torment. The soul had to accept this. But the young woman whom she so wisely counselled drooped her head and arms forlornly to the ground. No words, however wise, could explain the awfulness of death, not while the living were firmly attached to love, child-bearing, child-rearing, hunger, struggle, and the sunrise of tomorrow. Life had to flow all the time, for the living, like water in a stream. Makhaya held it in his hand. It was the little bundle of wood carvings. Yet he stood where he was until the two women slowly became aware of his presence.

"Makhaya!" Paulina exclaimed, jumping up and rushing towards the faint outline of his white shirt. "Oh, why did you take so long to come," she cried brokenly, and a torrent of hot tears spilled on to his shirt like a small waterfall. He slipped one free arm around her thin, bony waist.

"Aren't you glad I've come now? Don't cry. I've brought you something."

But even when she had untied the bundle near the firelight, with trembling fingers, this small waterfall continued to drench her arms and blouse and skirt. Mma-Millipede had to join in too with long, slow teardrops and many "Bathos" while they examined the carvings, one by one. After a time Makhaya could see that they were actually laughing in spite of those tears because they both knew the boy, with his oversized scarecrow coat and big smile. They saw how he had killed a snake in the bush, brought it back to his hut and carefully copied the patterns of its body on to the wooden handle of a porridge spoon. But the handwork on the little crocodile was different from the small boy's rough strokes. It had the smooth, polished finish of an old professional hunter and wood-carver and such a man had passed by the small boy's cattlepost one day and exchanged his own professional work for that of a cheerful little boy. And what other way was there to mourn the death of such a boy? Makhaya liked it this way, for he imagined the small boy the way he had been, standing quite close by and observing it. It made his heart feel very peaceful. It reminded Mma-Millipede that her back was aching and she was very tired. He stood up and accompanied Mma-Millipede all the way to her home, her tired feet shuffling quietly on the path beside him.

She sighed deeply to herself in an absent-minded way, but as they were about to part company she said, "Well, I say, my son, this is a world full of sorrows."

"Yes," he said.

But in spite of agreeing with Mma-Millipede his heart continued to feel peaceful. Perhaps he would have the courage to make children in such a world. For in this kind of lull from the inner torture of his life, he could think clearly. He was just an ordinary man and he wanted to stay that way all his life. None of the tinsel and glitter of the world attracted him but just what there was to live on and make do with in a village like Golema Mmidi. They were going to start shooting up everything one day, and George Appleby-Smith would come to him and say, "I'm sorry, but the government wants you to leave because you're a security risk."

And you wouldn't know what they meant by that because Africa was your country and there was no place else where a black man would come into his own and eventually lift up his head with dignity. Perhaps the whole world would still pretend not to understand your state of mind.

"We're morality," they'll say. "For God's sake stop the slaughter, we're on your side. We're morality and we're on your side."

But in the meanwhile he walked back to a firelight in the Botswana bush with these unending tortures stilled for a bit. He hoped to find out something because there were too many riddles and ironies these days, even in the African bush. He understood a man like Gilbert perfectly, as though life never did anything haphazardly but prepared people for their friends and threw them together at the right moment for some more obscure purpose than building dams, tobacco co-operatives, and cattle feeding grounds. Maybe he would not survive with his "security risk" status, but the world would not rid itself of African men. He would always be there, but not any longer as the white man's joke, or his "mundt" or his "kaffir" or his "boy".

Chapter 12

A week after Paulina Sebeso's child had been found dead in the hut at the cattlepost, the village of Golema Mmidi awoke to a day such as they would never forget. Looking back, the people even wondered aloud as to how it had all begun with such an ordinary event as the sunrise. Most of the women were up and about at dawn these days as they now had husbands to attend to, and from every yard a smoke haze arose as they all prepared the early morning tea and porridge.

Paulina found she had to wear two faces these days, one for when she was in a crowd and one for when she was alone. When she was alone, she smiled to herself because she was happy and could not reconcile this happiness to the loss of her boy and all her cattle. Mma-Millipede would have said that it was one rare occasion when the Lord took away with one hand and gave with another because it was seldom that the Lord ever gave a woman a man like Makhaya. Of course, Makhaya still observed some African customs like just coming and staying with a woman without first marrying her and then being indefinite about the date of marriage which might take place even after two or three children had been born. But which African man really loved a woman the way they could all see that Gilbert loved Maria? By love a man stuck to one woman, but African men liked the woman who stayed up the hill and the one in the valley and the one in the next village, all in the same nice indiscriminate way. In this way Makhaya differed from all African men, so Paulina reasoned. He had a lot of funny things to say for himself too, not all of which she understood, but she would have fought anyone with blows who questioned her loyalty to Makhaya. So she made the tea with a gay, light heart and then set a pot near the fire for bathing water.

I'll have to do this and that today, she said to herself, nodding her head as she ticked off the items and carefully poured the tea into the cups. Makhaya had told her not to slosh any of it on to the saucer. Even homes of mud huts must be run like a hotel, he said, with everything spick-and-span, and the small girl ought to be bathed from head to toe every night. Talk about a wonderful man who cared about all these small things? Not only that. The tobacco the women were to grow had been the talk of the village ever since the men had come back.

They had all been to the farm to stare in fascination at the tiny experimental plot of olive-green tobacco leaf. So, this was what their wives and sweethearts were up to now, they said to each other, flushed with pride, the same way the ancient hunters of history must have reacted when they came back from hunting trips and found their wives had cultivated the wheat and domesticated a few wild animals for their meat. Indeed what else was this small venture into tobacco growing but to arouse an interest in the men in the production of cash crops. The men would eventually have to take on the task of producing those acres and acres of tobacco. But first they would have to stay home. Could a twenty-eight-mile fence be erected for a cattle holding ground, Gilbert had asked? Of course, they said. And the men were prepared to pool their labour for the big job, but just right now they were sorting out how to keep alive what cattle they had left. This was problem number one until help arrived, three weeks from now, in the form of emergency rations and a spare borehole.

Paulina saw Gilbert walking into the yard now to

fetch Makhaya so that they could go to the ranch. And Makhaya was still asleep even though she had awakened him fifteen minutes ago. He seemed to like getting up in a commotion of hurry. Paulina rushed about flustered and breathless for five minutes until the two men walked out of the yard. Then she bent down, poured the remainder of the bath into a basin, picked it up, and was about to enter the hut to wash when, to her amazement, she saw a silent figure crouched down near the entrance of her yard. It was one of Matenge's servants.

"Good-day, friend," she said apprehensively. "What do you need?"

The servant looked up, a sly grin on her servile face. "I am sent to bring you to court. The chief has a case."

"I?" Paulina said, stupefied. "But what have I done?"

Again there was that sly grin. This wretched creature in smelly rags and tatters was the last contact with mankind that Matenge had. He had been muttering and fuming to the servants for some days now, and the grinning was an arrogant pride of someone who is always kicked around yet needed by the master.

"You ought to know what you've been up to," the servant said. "All I can say is that I am sent."

"Agh, leave me alone," Paulina said impatiently, and walked into the hut.

But when she came out the servant was still there, crouched down, and she began to be afraid, wondering what she had done to offend Matenge. And all she could think of was that she had forgotten to report the death of her son to the chief. It was a custom but surely a court case could not be made out of forgetfulness? She even pulled the little girl about roughly as she dressed her for school, so nervous and unsettled did she feel. Also, today was the day when she and a group of women were to harvest the first batch of tobacco. They would soon join her in her yard. She turned to the servant, wanting to wait for her friends.

"I suppose the chief is offended because I forgot to report the death of my son?" she asked tentatively.

"I really don't know," the servant said, with that maddening grin.

Paulina decided that she would no longer speak to this dreadful person but she took her time, dishing up a plate of porridge for herself and her child, waiting for her friends. She liked company at all times, especially when there was trouble.

Just at this time too, the six old men who sat on the village council were receiving the message to attend court and, like Paulina, they were stunned and apprehensive. Matenge never called them unless it was to destroy an inhabitant of Golema Mmidi. He had never done one act of kindness towards the villagers, seeming to be placed there only for their torture. They gathered their tattered coats about them and shuffled towards the centre of the village.

Paulina's friends stepped into the yard at that moment and straight away decided to accompany Paulina to the court case. Along the way they picked up Maria, then Dinorego, and Mma Millipede. The news travelled swiftly from hut to hut, and men and women immediately set down their chores for the day and made their way to the village centre. They were even excited in a silent way as though they had known this day would arrive when they would all face their persecutor of many years.

They had been straining together in one direction for years, and Matenge had been straining in the opposite direction, always pulling them down. Because of this they had politely avoided him, but today they wanted to see his face when their cattle were dying while his cattle were safe, way up on the northern border where a river flowed the year round and the grass was good and salty and green. They wanted to see this man who had all the privileges, who had never known a day of starvation in this country of two years of good rain and seven years of drought. They wanted to know what his mood was like after these years of silence and mute disagreement. They wanted him to know they were not after his Chevrolet or big house. They would even tell him this with gentle smiles and pleasant gestures and reassure him that it was only their lives they wanted to set right and he must not stand in their way. He was there through their tolerance. They would even be able to tolerate ten thousand Matenges, but the disagreement between him and them was that he said no, no, no, to everything they wanted to do. But they were the people of Golema Mmidi to whom too many tyrants and unscrupulous men had said no, no, no, and people like the people of Golema Mmidi could not be hunted, hounded, banished, and persecuted forever and forever and forever. Were they to be driven to the vultures who now soared overhead in the blazing, dead-white sky? Very well then, the whole village, as one man, would go and die in the bush if that was all a tyrant wanted of them. If you said no, no, no, and kept your claws in a people's heart, what else did you want but that they should all die? You were so unreasonable.

These thoughts ran through the minds of all the villagers as they hurried towards the home of Matenge. It wasn't any longer Paulina Sebeso who was to be persecuted alone but the whole village of Golema Mmidi. Thus, when all the villagers suddenly found themselves meeting face to face at the village centre, they looked at each other and smiled and laughed with a load taken off their minds because they were at last of the same mind. Only three people were absent—Gilbert, Makhaya, and Pelotona, the permit man.

Matenge had not expected this. He stood in the shadow of his enclosed porch, watching the crowd. When they turned and walked towards the gate of his yard, he retreated indoors, in panic, running from window to window and door to door, barricading himself inside. The servants, observing his panic, crept like stricken shadows out of the back door and fled into the bush. He was left alone with his panic in a dark, locked house. He walked to one of the windows and looked down into the yard. The villagers had all seated themselves on the ground, with their faces turned expectantly towards the house, waiting for him to come out. And they would wait and wait and wait now because this was the end of the road for them and Matenge. Big, slow tears rolled down the rutted grooves of his cheeks as he stood there, watching them.

Why did he cry? The greatest moments of his life had been when he had inflicted suffering on his fellow men. People were not people to him but things he kicked about, pawns to be used by him, to break, banish and destroy for his entertainment. That was the tradition in which he had grown up, and maybe he could not be blamed for taking full advantage of it. Most chiefs were half Matenge and half of the casual charm of his brother, and they lived on their own weird tightrope as fathers of the people. Half the time they turned on the charm, just in the nick of time to save themselves from damnation. But they were all an evil, cruel crowd. Only Matenge had not known how to turn on the charm to save himself.

Was he crying now because, for the first time in his life, he was feeling what it must be like to face a tomorrow without any future? That was what those upturned faces meant. He would have to go away. They weren't going to tolerate a man like him any longer because he would not give way nor understand that they needed co-operation from the man at the top to whom everyone had to go for permission to progress. The Matenges and Paramount Chief Sekotos did not have to lift up the spades and dig the earth. It cost them nothing to say, yes, yes, yes, build your dam because we have no water in this country. But it gave them a deep and perverted joy to say no, no, no. The end of it was that Matenge had to barricade himself up, not because the villagers were about to rise up and tear him to shreds, but because he was an evil pervert and knew it. Only you could not understand why a man like that stood there crying like a forlorn and lonely child.

A flock of vultures gathered overhead, circling in the sky, eyeing the villagers with extreme interest and curiosity, so accustomed had they become to feasting on anything in sight, and it was the long, lazy, swooping flight of the vultures over the centre of the village that confirmed to the three men at the cattle ranch that something had gone seriously wrong in the village of Golemo Mmidi. They had been waiting for the village men to come to the ranch. Cattle had to be trucked, rations distributed. But all that had faced them for a half an hour of waiting was this eerie silence. Then the flight of the vultures. Gilbert and Makhaya and the permit man looked at each other as much as to say: What now? Then they walked along the footpaths, passed the deserted huts with rising alarm. No Paulina. No Maria. And even the farm workers had left off their duties.

The three men got into the Land-Rover and drove to the village centre and right up to the gate of Matenge's home. They climbed out a little uncertainly and stood near the gate. Everyone turned around but for a while no one spoke. And there was just this silent, shut-up house with the gleaming Chevrolet in the yard. Even Dinorego failed to explain the situation, and once more the villagers turned their heads towards the house.

"What's happening here, people?" Makhaya asked at last, in a loud, clear voice.

"We're waiting for the chief to come out, son," Dinorego replied, without turning around.

How long had this strange game been going on, Makhaya wondered? Without further thought, he began walking calmly towards the house. He climbed the steep flight of stairs and disappeared from the gaze of the villagers on the dark, enclosed porch. A moment later they heard a tremendous crash as Makhaya broke down the door. Then a long silence. The villagers all arose and also climbed the steep stairway. Those in the forefront stood looking silently for a while into the big dining room, not at the luxurious couches, carpets and high-backed kingly chair, but at the dead, still body hanging from a rafter. Makhaya had the phone in his hand and was talking to George Appleby-Smith.

"I can't say for how long," he was saying. "Must I cut the rope?"

"Are you sure he's dead?" the inspector asked.

"I can't say," Makhaya faltered. "I'm not sure, except that he's quite still."

Makhaya paused and a twisted spasm of pain swept across his face. Could the man hang like that with all the villagers staring in?

"There's been some trouble here today," he continued on the phone. "I don't know the details, but the whole village is here."

"Okay, cut down the body. I'll be there in about ten minutes," and Makhaya heard the man at the other end slam down the phone.

In his office George Appleby-Smith stared sightlessly at the wall. Things always went this way in this goddam country. Every village was a hornets' nest where someone had to be irrevocably got rid of. Someone had to go round the bend, die, or be driven out. Life was always extremes, harsh blacks and whites with no soft greys or in-betweens or compromises. He'd long seen Matenge was a crack but in this kind of goddam country where everyone was bullshitting around, the cracks and nuts and loose bolts had the upper hand. Even his good friend Paramount Chief Sekoto was a crack and nut and loose bolt. He smiled to himself. Today, after it was all over, he'd go and have a quiet beer in the railway pub—to a fellow whose guts he admired. He hadn't thought Gilbert would stick it out to the end. He'd long expected him to become a loose bolt too, with all the nonsense that was going on in Golema Mmidi.

He picked up the phone, still smiling to himself. A moment later he heard the gay, bubbling voice of the Paramount Chief, "Hullo, hullo, George. How's things?"

"Have you got a coffin, pal?"

"Ha, ha. Gracious me, George. Don't tell me you want to die now. You're just a spring chicken."

"It's not me," said that familiar, casual drawl. "It's your brother Matenge. He's gone and killed himself."

There was an abrupt silence at the other end, and George could quite clearly see Chief Sekoto put on his funeral face. Chief Sekoto was a play actor on all occasions. He lived life with his face while his heart remained calm, empty, and serene.

"I'm very sorry to hear this news, George," he said.

"So am I," George said dryly.

"I'm coming right over with the coffin," Chief Sekoto said. But he remained holding on to the phone in an absent-minded way. How many beasts would have to be slaughtered? How many relatives to insult by not sending a personal invitation to the funeral? How to squash the scandal of the suicide? Oh, oh, the mess and fuss and bother. The talk, talk, talk. He closed his eyes. Even in death his brother upset his digestion for the whole day. He put the phone down, dusted his hands and waddled briskly out of the office, carefully adjusting his funeral face. Along the way to his home he met his secretary.

"Pule," he said, in a sombre voice. "Please order a coffin. Put it in the truck. I'll have to go to Golema Mmidi as brother has just died of a heart attack."

He said this to several people, even the wife. Matenge had died of a heart attack. He wanted to create confusion. The people of Golema Mmidi would come up with their own story, but once there were two conflicting versions, people would doubt everything, even if they saw the rope around Matenge's neck. And they would soon become bored. But a suicide, in a chief's house? Oh, oh, oh. It would go down in history. Most of all, things had to go smoothly, quickly. Chief Sekoto had lots of practice too. He buried everyone—concubines, commoners, royal relatives, and foreigners. And he put his funeral face away one hour after the dust of the earth had enclosed the coffin. This time there was a heavy feeling in his heart. It wasn't easy to dismiss the intense, dramatic face of his brother. As though it was a question mark before life. As though his brother had suffered because he had wanted more things than a man should desire for one life and then life itself had frustrated all these desires. As though his brother had been the helpless victim of terrible, private hungers. What else made a man do all the things his brother had done? And a great shadow of gloom clouded Chief Sekoto's outlook that day. By the time he arrived in Golema Mmidi, he wasn't play acting any more but was genuinely upset.

He found the villagers still seated quietly and patiently in the yard as he drove the big truck with the coffin through the gate. A few men moved to the truck to lift down the coffin and carry it into the house. Chief Sekoto got out and stood for a moment leaning against the truck, trying to take stock of the situation. There was that desperately earnest young man, Gilbert, also leaning against his Land-Rover and looking up at the sky where the vultures circled and circled. Chief Sekoto could picture so clearly the day Gilbert had walked into his office and Chief Sekoto had thought him mad with all his talk about the poor. The poor were just the poor, and the commoner was just the commoner, and they were not very interesting people to Chief Sekoto. They lived such stupid lazy lives. They were so filthy in their habits that a mud hut was all they deserved.

How was Chief Sekoto to know that there was a quiet and desperate revolution going on throughout the whole wide world? People were being drawn closer and closer to each other as brothers, and once you looked on the other man as your brother, you could not bear that he should want for anything or live in darkness. Maybe he knew nothing about this because this revolution belonged to young people like Gilbert and Makhaya.

These young people only puzzled a man like Chief Sekoto. If he had had the good looks of the handsome refugee what a colourful drama his life would have been! One dramatic love affair after another. And here was the young man, wasting his life away in the bush. Someone told him they did this because they were communists—all this permission requested to build dams and register co-operatives. He had queried his friend George about this communist business, and his only reply had been: Bullshit. George had all the top-secret information too, and Chief Sekoto never doubted his word. Besides there were mad people and mad people. He had never lost a night's sleep over the presence of the two young men in his tribal reserve, but he had lost plenty of sleep over his brother.

He straightened his short body and waddled briskly up the stairs. There was a crowd of people in the big dining room and the coffin was on the floor. He averted his gaze from the body of his brother, which was stretched out on a couch, and walked over to George, who stood by himself at the far end of the room.

"What happened?" he asked in a whisper.

George shrugged. "People say they wanted to have a peaceful discussion with the chief," he said, keeping his face expressionless.

"What was this peaceful discussion about?" Chief Sekoto asked.

"Their cattle are dying," George said, then just kept silent.

Chief Sekoto looked at him, puzzled. "I don't understand," he said. "Did my brother kill himself because people's cattle are dying?"

George gave his friend a long look before replying, then he shrugged again. "Just a week ago," he said softly, ". . . just a week ago we found a dead child of this village at the cattle post. He died a most horrible death from malnutrition. We held no one to blame for it because you can't prosecute droughts and famine. But today your brother wanted to prosecute the mother of this child for some unknown offence. The people of this village came to attend the trial. That's all they did."

Chief Sekoto looked at the ground. He did not know what to think because if he did he might have felt too, and that would stifle and choke him. It was all a bad tragedy, his brother, the poor. But George Appleby-Smith stared at everything with peaceful eyes, even the way the village men gently lifted the body of Matenge into the coffin. He would never be able to close his eyes to all these people in rags and tatters and no shoes. They were all he really lived with in his daily work. They were so poor, yet it never occurred to them to steal. Because of this the prisons were nearly always empty. A murder case turned up once in a blue moon. Instead, you found yourself inspector of a police station where a lot of absent-minded people walked in to report that they had forgotten their blankets on the train. Could you please find their blankets? You got other curious things happening to you, too. Once, for a year, almost at the exact same hour each afternoon, a big white goat would step into his office and walk around sniffing the untidy jumble of papers. Then walk out again. He never found out to whom that goat belonged because he never directly involved himself with anyone, but both goats and people love George Appleby-Smith. And he appreciated this deeply.

The men lifted the coffin and carried it out to the truck. A lot of the villagers, including Mma-Millipede and Dinorego, had decided to accompany Paramount Chief Sekoto and would stay over in his village for the funeral. The rest of the dazed and stunned villagers slowly began to make their way homeward, still unable to utter a word. You have to be loved a bit by the time you die. People can only say good things about the dead, and if you've left no treasures on this earth, what's there to hold on to except a terrible pity? Perhaps the people of Golema Mmidi were afraid, too, that they had really killed Matenge, in a strange gathering-together of all their wills. It was as if they did not want an evil to impose itself on them, and they had all quickly and silently decided to suppress it.

They found it difficult now to break the cohesion and singleness of purpose that had drawn them together that day. Until later that night they kept on grouping and regrouping in each other's yards, drinking bowls of sour milk porridge, discussing the weather and how hot it had been that day. But not once did they mention the name of Matenge, though he was in all their thoughts, hovering like a great, unseen shadow over the whole village.

This strange mental disassociation from the events of the day also took place in Gilbert, Makhaya, and Pelotona, the permit man, when they arrived back at the farm for a late lunch together. They held some half-hearted, distracted conversation about rationing water until the emergency borehole had been sunk. But they lapsed into unexpected intervals of silence. You couldn't ever forget Matenge, not once you had met him face to face and he had spat his venom out at you. Matenge made you doubt the basic goodness of mankind. He made you think of all the people who are only half like him, and this completely shattered the innocence and trust with which you might approach fairly harmless people who do a bit of evil now and then to entertain themselves.

Gilbert had been roughed up inside more than all of them. He had had to do a complete somersault of thought and feeling after his arrival in Golema Mmidi. No one had told him there was such a thing as an African oppressor, nor had he expected to find a Matenge exploiting his own people through the cattle speculating business. Hundreds of white men did it and were continuing to do it with efficient ease in Botswana. But an African robbing Africans? And he had tortured himself through many sleepless nights at the ease with which he had destroyed Matenge's cattle speculating business. There were other things too—the pathetic way in which Matenge always backed down when confronted by a superior.

But if a man like Gilbert had really kept his mind on the Matenges who were an inverted whirlpool of seething intrigues, on the crazy semi-literate politicians like Joas Tsepe, he might have overlooked the kind of people almost everyone overlooked—the Dinoregos and Mma-Millipedes. At the most bitter times of Gilbert's stay in Golema Mmidi, Dinorego had always said: "I think the Good God don't like it." But he said it as though the "Good God" was quite nearby, listening, observing, and Dinorego, his screwed-up face listening to the "Good God", was what had made Gilbert stay and stay. And he mixed it all up with a thousand and one things: the way he smelled the summer rain on the far, flat horizon, four or five months before the first, fat globs of raindrops fell two by two, three by three on the parched earth. Enormous thunderstorms brewed and boiled on these far off horizons, but it never rained and people never ploughed, until one unsuspecting day it rained in sheets and so hard that the roar of the rain drowned out the volcanic thunderclaps.

What was he looking for? What was he doing? Agriculture? The need for a poor country to catch up with the Joneses in the rich countries? Should super-highways and skyscrapers replace the dusty footpaths and thorn scrub? It might be what he said he had in mind; at least, he said this to excuse himself for the need to live in a hurricane of activity. But the real life he had lived for three years had been dominated by the expression on Dinorego's face, and God and agriculture were all mixed up together after these three years. Yet it was a real God this who stalked his footsteps along the dusty pathways, who listened with quiet interest to the discussions on agriculture. Gilbert had no clear explanation of how he had become certain of this, but there was a feeling of great goodness in this country.

But Mma-Millipede had the beginnings of an answer as to why everything was so mixed up. She had traced the course of man's whole destiny through her studies of the wandering tribes of Israel. Sometimes a man's God was like Solomon and he decked himself up in gold and he built a house that was a hundred cubits in length and fifty cubits in breadth and thirty cubits in height. Gold candlesticks, cherubims, and pomegranates adorned this house, which had forty bathrooms. And there were bowls and snuffers and spoons and censers and door hinges of pure gold. All that the followers of Solomon could do was to gape and marvel and chronicle these wonders in minute detail. Even Solomon's wisdom took secondary place to his material possessions and dazzling raiments. Then came a God who was greater than Solomon, but he walked around with no shoes, in rough cloth, wandering up and down the dusty footpaths in the hot sun, with no bed on which to rest his head. And all that the followers of this God could do was to chonicle, in minute detail, the wonder and marvel of his wisdom.

There were two such destinies which faced Africa—that of the followers of Solomon and that of a man with no shoes. But the man with no shoes had been bypassed, scorned, and ridiculed while the Solomons stalked the land in their golden Chevrolets. Who would eat then if all the gold and pomegranates went into the house of Solomon? Who would bathe if all the water went into his forty bathrooms? Who would have time to plough if everyone had to join the parade to watch Solomon pass by in his Chevrolet of molten gold, his top hat and silk shirt, glittering in the African sun? For that's all that Solomon wants—a lot of gapers and marvellers. And things were mixed up because there were too many Solomons and too many men with no shoes, and no one could be certain who would win out in the end—except that the man with no shoes was often too hungry to stand in the parade these days.

And that was what it boiled down to in the end—a silent and fascinating battle between the Solomons and aspiring Solomons like Joas Tsepe, and the God with no shoes. The Solomons made the most noise in the world, hopping from one international conference to another, bowing and scraping to the left and right. But the God with no shoes continued to live where he always had—in the small brown birds of the bush, in the dusty footpaths, and in the expressions of thin old men in tattered coats. He was just wondering what all the fuss and clamour was about, you know, these international brotherhoods, the sounding brass and tinkling cymbals, because he really owned the world and the fish in the ocean. It amused him to see all these fellows strutting about, with no humility, forever scheming and plotting to gain what would never be theirs.

The way this God with no shoes carried on might easily delude you into thinking he was a charming halfwit like Paramount Chief Sekoto or hesitant about truth like Mma-Millipede or tortured and tormented like Makhaya. He changed about from day to day contradicting and confusing himself by all he had to learn, never certain of anything the way the fortune-tellers were. He had upset Makhaya this day by stacking the cards one way and then toppling them another. He had packed all these cards up in a precarious pyramid and stood by while Matenge picked off the topmost card. It would have been different had Matenge really victimized Paulina for whatever he wanted to victimize her for. Maybe her association with Makhaya. But then a man like Makhaya would not have stood by with tied hands.

He would have had blood on his hands by now and been in some cell, with George Appleby-Smith lecturing him on how he had let him down. But the God with no shoes, with his queer, inverted reasoning, had brought Makhaya, a real and potential murderer, face to face with the body of Matenge just hanging there and hanging there.

"Don't you see?" he said softly. "Murder is small-minded business."

Did you really trust a God like that? He made you take a long and perilous journey along a road where everyone threw things at you. Then he said you were small-minded if you wanted to throw things back. Why didn't he do something about the throwers then? Because one Matenge died and another replaced him, and no matter which way you turned there was always a Matenge there to throw something at you. And Makhaya knew that that day was always ahead of him. He would come face to face with one of these grinning, ghoulish oppressors and have nowhere to run any more. And he would just lift up his arm and knock him dead with a mighty blow, right between his grinning eyes. And he might turn round to this invisible God who tormented his life with question after question and knock him down too. Someone had to go into oblivion—either a Makhaya or the oppressor. And Makhaya did not mind if it was he. Because a man could not go on taking it, all the filth and lies and hypocrisy. He might like to step right out of it into a black, silent death, never to live again.

"What are you thinking about, Mack?" Gilbert asked, at last, in a tired, depressed voice.

Makhaya raised his hands with a helpless gesture. "I don't know," he said. "I don't know if I'm thinking at all."

It was this quiet, hollow feeling inside all of them that made them feel so low. It was as though they had strained so hard against a heavy, unyielding door, only to find it wasn't there any more. They could not, all at once, total up the good things in this struggle, how it had made them true comrades, how they would not ever have clarified their ideas had they not lived under the shadow of blind opposition. These things would come with tomorrow, when all the hard work had to be done and even Makhaya would find, in spite of himself, that he had to live and give up his morbid speculations on oppressors and oppressed. Even this Good God whom Dinorego said was "everywhere about" stood watching them that evening with an amused look in his eye. Why didn't Gilbert talk about how exciting irrigation farming would be in Golema Mmidi? Everyone would want to do it now. Just look at the way everyone was shocked out of their minds! Did this fellow Gilbert think progress was as easy as learning to drive a tractor? People had to be given shock after shock to wake them up good and thoroughly, and preparations for progress took place long before progress even started. As for the oppressors! Did you mean Joas Tsepe would win the election as councillor for Golema Mmidi? Maybe anywhere else but not in Golema Mmidi. They would much prefer Mma-Millipede, who mixed up spiritual counselling with practical advice and whom the Good God had long prepared for this position. In fact, there was not anything he would not do for a village like Golema Mmidi, which was a place he had especially set aside to bring all his favourite people together. He wanted them to show everyone else just how quickly things could really change, how ordinary people could get up and do things for themselves and produce enough for their needs and have some left over for sale. But why were they all so boring this evening? Ah, but he was a little bored too. His favourite mouthpiece, Dinorego, was away at the funeral.

Therefore the Good God cast one last look at Makhaya, whom he intended revenging almightily for his silent threat to knock him down. He would so much entangle this stupid young man with marriage and babies and children that he would always have to think, not twice but several hundred times, before he came to knocking anyone down.

He wandered along the footpath, in the direction of the sunset, and stopped for a while in the yard of Paulina Sebeso. She was busy at her smoke haze fire, preparing supper, but she paused and looked up expectantly as she heard familiar footsteps. It was Makhaya coming home. His long dismal train of thought made him overlook the still, glorious ball of hot, red light which hung in the sky. He was about to start saying those impractical things to Paulina, you know, like this world is not a fit place to live in, but she came rushing towards him with her hands outstretched because she had been deeply frightened at the way he had walked up the steps of Matenge's house, as if he would just be swallowed up by a monster and would not mind. He was like the wind or a fluid substance you could not hold on to. She grasped hold of his hands with that half-laughing, half-puzzled expression, perhaps even shocked to feel that his hands were large, solid bone, slightly warm and damp. He was solid all over, strong and muscular, but the inside of him, the expression of his face was so strange and unreal. What did you say to such a man?

She asked, "Will you have some food?"

He smiled. She was the best of all woman he had known—no sulks, no dead eyes, no dead anything about her.

"So much has happened so quickly," he said. "I forgot to ask you if you'd like to marry me. Will you, Paulie?"

After all, he had said he wanted to marry someone.

Didn't he? But even though Paulina said yes a bit too quickly, she hardly believed it. As though everything was uncertain, new and strange and beginning from scratch.

Related Readings

CONTENTS

The Rain Came

by Grace Ogot

*When drought threatens the very
existence of a village, can anything be
done to make rain fall? And if so, what
price are people willing to pay to bring
that life-giving rain? In this short story by
Kenyan-born Grace Ogot, a chief's
daughter learns what that price must be.*

The chief was still far from the gate when his
daughter Oganda saw him. She ran to meet him.
Breathlessly she asked her father, "What is the news,
great Chief? Everyone in the village is anxiously
waiting to hear when it will rain." Labong'o held out
his hands for his daughter but he did not say a word.
Puzzled by her father's cold attitude Oganda ran back
to the village to warn the others that the chief was
back.

The atmosphere in the village was tense and
confused. Everyone moved aimlessly and fussed in the
yard without actually doing any work. A young
woman whispered to her co-wife, "If they have not
solved this rain business today, the chief will crack."
They had watched him getting thinner and thinner as
the people kept on pestering him. "Our cattle lie dying
in the fields," they reported. "Soon it will be our
children and then ourselves. Tell us what to do to save
our lives, oh great Chief." So the chief had daily
prayed with the Almighty through the ancestors to
deliver them from their distress.

Instead of calling the family together and giving

them the news immediately, Labong'o went to his own hut, a sign that he was not to be disturbed. Having replaced the shutter, he sat in the dimly-lit hut to contemplate.

It was no longer a question of being the chief of hunger-stricken people that weighed Labong'o's heart. It was the life of his only daughter that was at stake. At the time when Oganda came to meet him, he saw the glittering chain shining around her waist. The prophecy was complete. "It is Oganda, Oganda, my only daughter, who must die so young." Labong'o burst into tears before finishing the sentence. The chief must not weep. Society had declared him the bravest of men. But Labong'o did not care any more. He assumed the position of a simple father and wept bitterly. He loved his people, the Luo, but what were the Luo for him without Oganda? Her life had brought a new life in Labong'o's world and he ruled better than he could remember. How would the spirit of the village survive his beautiful daughter? "There are so many homes and so many parents who have daughters. Why choose this one? She is all I have." Labong'o spoke as if the ancestors were there in the hut and he could see them face to face. Perhaps they were there, warning him to remember his promise on the day he was enthroned when he said aloud, before the elders, "I will lay down life, if necessary, and the life of my household, to save this tribe from the hands of the enemy." "Deny! Deny!" he could hear the voice of his forefathers mocking him.

When Labong'o was consecrated chief he was only a young man. Unlike his father, he ruled for many years with only one wife. But people rebuked him because his only wife did not bear him a daughter. He married a second, a third, and a fourth wife, but they all gave birth to male children. When Labong'o married a fifth wife she bore him a daughter. They called her Oganda, meaning "beans", because her skin was very fair. Out of Labong'o's twenty children, Oganda was the only girl. Though she was the chief's favourite, her mother's co-wives swallowed their jealous feelings and showered her with love. After all, they said, Oganda was a female child whose days in the royal family were numbered. She would soon marry at a tender age and leave the enviable position to someone else.

Never in his life had he been faced with such an impossible decision. Refusing to yield to the rain-maker's request would mean sacrificing the whole tribe, putting the interests of the individual above those of the society. More than that. It would mean disobeying the ancestors, and most probably wiping the Luo people from the surface of the earth. On the other hand, to let Oganda die as a ransom for the people would permanently cripple Labong'o spiritually. He knew he would never be the same chief again.

The words of Ndithi, the medicine man, still echoed in his ears. "Podho, the ancestor of the Luo, appeared to me in a dream last night, and he asked me to speak to the chief and the people," Ndithi had said to the gathering of tribesmen. "A young woman who has not known a man must die so that the country may have rain. While Podho was still talking to me, I saw a young woman standing at the lakeside, her hands raised, above her head. Her skin was as fair as the skin of young deer in the wilderness. Her tall slender figure stood like a lonely reed at the river bank. Her sleepy eyes wore a sad look like that of a bereaved mother. She wore a gold ring on her left ear, and a glittering brass chain around her waist. As I still marvelled at the beauty of this young woman, Podho told me, 'Out of all the women in this land, we have chosen this one. Let her offer herself as a sacrifice to the lake monster! And on that day, the rain will come down in torrents.

Let everyone stay at home on that day, lest he be carried away by the floods.'"

Outside there was a strange stillness, except for the thirsty birds that sang lazily on the dying trees. The blinding mid-day heat had forced the people to retire to their huts. Not far away from the chief's hut, two guards were snoring away quietly. Labong'o removed his crown and the large eagle-head that hung loosely on his shoulders. He left the hut, and instead of asking Nyabog'o the messenger to beat the drum, he went straight and beat it himself. In no time the whole household had assembled under the siala tree where he usually addressed them. He told Oganda to wait a while in her grandmother's hut.

When Labong'o stood to address his household, his voice was hoarse and the tears choked him. He started to speak, but words refused to leave his lips. His wives and sons knew there was great danger. Perhaps their enemies had declared war on them. Labong'o's eyes were red, and they could see he had been weeping. At last he told them. "One whom we love and treasure must be taken away from us. Oganda is to die." Labong'o's voice was so faint, that he could not hear it himself. But he continued, "The ancestors have chosen her to be offered as a sacrifice to the lake monster in order that we may have rain."

They were completely stunned. As a confused murmur broke out, Oganda's mother fainted and was carried off to her own hut. But the other people rejoiced. They danced around singing and chanting, "Oganda is the lucky one to die for the people. If it is to save the people, let Oganda go."

In her grandmother's hut Oganda wondered what the whole family were discussing about her that she could not hear. Her grandmother's hut was well away from the chief's court and, much as she strained her ears, she could not hear what was said. "It must be marriage," she concluded. It was an accepted custom for the family to discuss their daughter's future marriage behind her back. A faint smile played on Oganda's lips as she thought of the several young men who swallowed saliva at the mere mention of her name.

There was Kech, the son of a neighbouring clan elder. Kech was very handsome. He had sweet, meek eyes and a roaring laughter. He would make a wonderful father, Oganda thought. But they would not be a good match. Kech was a bit too short to be her husband. It would humiliate her to have to look down at Kech each time she spoke to him. Then she thought of Dimo, the tall young man who had already distinguished himself as a brave warrior and an outstanding wrestler. Dimo adored Oganda, but Oganda thought he would make a cruel husband, always quarrelling and ready to fight. No, she did not like him. Oganda fingered the glittering chain on her waist as she thought of Osinda. A long time ago when she was quite young Osinda had given her that chain, and instead of wearing it around her neck several times, she wore it round her waist where it could stay permanently. She heard her heart pounding so loudly as she thought of him. She whispered, "Let it be you they are discussing, Osinda, the lovely one. Come now and take me away . . ."

The lean figure in the doorway startled Oganda, who was rapt in thought about the man she loved. "You have frightened me, Grandma," said Oganda laughing. "Tell me, is it my marriage you are discussing? You can take it from me that I won't marry any of them." A smile played on her lips again. She was coaxing the old lady to tell her quickly, to tell her they were pleased with Osinda.

In the open space outside the excited relatives were dancing and singing. They were coming to the hut now, each carrying a gift to put at Oganda's feet. As their singing got nearer Oganda was able to hear what they were saying: "If it is to save the people, if it is to give us rain, let Oganda go. Let Oganda die for her people, and for her ancestors." Was she mad to think that they were singing about her? How could she die? She found the lean figure of her grandmother barring the door. She could not get out. The look on her grandmother's face warned her that there was danger around the corner. "Mother, it is not marriage then?" Oganda asked urgently. She suddenly felt panicky like a mouse cornered by a hungry cat. Forgetting that there was only one door in the hut Oganda fought desperately to find another exit. She must fight for her life. But there was none.

She closed her eyes, leapt like a wild tiger through the door, knocking her grandmother flat to the ground. There outside in mourning garments Labong'o stood motionless, his hands folded at the back. He held his daughter's hand and led her away from the excited crowd to the little red-painted hut where her mother was resting. Here he broke the news officially to his daughter.

For a long time the three souls who loved one another dearly sat in darkness. It was no good speaking. And even if they tried, the words could not have come out. In the past they had been like three cooking stones, sharing their burdens. Taking Oganda away from them would leave two useless stones which would not hold a cooking-pot.

News that the beautiful daughter of the chief was to be sacrificed to give the people rain spread across the country like wind. At sunset the chief's village was full of relatives and friends who had come to congratulate Oganda. Many more were on their way coming, carrying their gifts. They would dance till morning to keep her company. And in the morning they would prepare her a big farewell feast. All these relatives thought it a great honour to be selected by the spirits to die, in order that the society may live. "Oganda's name will always remain a living name among us," they boasted.

But was it maternal love that prevented Minya from rejoicing with the other women? Was it the memory of the agony and pain of child-birth that made her feel so sorrowful? Or was it the deep warmth and understanding that passes between a suckling babe and her mother that made Oganda part of her life, her flesh? Of course it was an honour, a great honour, for her daughter to be chosen to die for the country. But what could she gain once her daughter was blown away by the wind? There were so many other women in the land, why choose her daughter, her only child! Had human life any meaning at all — other women had houses full of children while she, Minya, had to lose her only child!

In the cloudless sky the moon shone brightly, and the numerous stars glittered with a bewitching beauty. The dancers of all age-groups assembled to dance before Oganda, who sat close to her mother, sobbing quietly. All these years she had been with her people she thought she understood them. But now she discovered that she was a stranger among them. If they loved her as they had always professed why were they not making any attempt to save her? Did her people really understand what it felt like to die young? Unable to restrain her emotions any longer, she sobbed loudly as her age-group got up to dance. They were young and beautiful and very soon they would marry and have their own children. They would have husbands to love and little huts for themselves. They would have reached maturity. Oganda touched the chain around her waist as she thought of Osinda. She wished Osinda was there too, among her friends.

"Perhaps he is ill," she thought gravely. The chain comforted Oganda — she would die with it around her waist and wear it in the underground world.

In the morning a big feast was prepared for Oganda. The women prepared many different tasty dishes so that she could pick and choose. "People don't eat after death," they said. Delicious though the food looked, Oganda touched none of it. Let the happy people eat. She contented herself with sips of water from a little calabash.

The time for her departure was drawing near, and each minute was precious. It was a day's journey to the lake. She was to walk all night, passing through the great forest. But nothing could touch her, not even the denizens of the forest. She was already anointed with sacred oil. From the time Oganda received the sad news she had expected Osinda to appear any moment. But he was not there. A relative told her that Osinda was away on a private visit. Oganda realized that she would never see her beloved again.

In the afternoon the whole village stood at the gate to say good-bye and to see her for the last time. Her mother wept on her neck for a long time. The great chief in a mourning skin came to the gate bare-footed, and mingled with the people — a simple father in grief. He took off his wrist bracelet and put it on his daughter's wrist saying, "You will always live among us. The spirit of our forefathers is with you."

Tongue-tied and unbelieving Oganda stood there before the people. She had nothing to say. She looked at her home once more. She could hear her heart beating so painfully within her. All her childhood plans were coming to an end. She felt like a flower nipped in the bud never to enjoy the morning dew again. She looked at her weeping mother, and whispered, "Whenever you want to see me, always look at the sunset. I will be there."

Oganda turned southwards to start her trek to the lake. Her parents, relatives, friends and admirers stood at the gate and watched her go.

Her beautiful slender figure grew smaller and smaller till she mingled with the thin dry trees in the forest. As Oganda walked the lonely path that wound its way in the wilderness, she sang a song, and her own voice kept her company.

> The ancestors have said Oganda must die
> The daughter of the chief must be sacrificed,
> When the lake monster feeds on my flesh.
> The people will have rain.
> Yes, the rain will come down in torrents.
> And the floods will wash away the sandy beaches
> When the daughter of the chief dies in the lake.
> My age-group has consented
> My parents have consented
> So have my friends and relatives.
> Let Oganda die to give us rain.
> My age-group are young and ripe,
> Ripe for womanhood and motherhood
> But Oganda must die young,
> Oganda must sleep with the ancestors.
> Yes, rain will come down in torrents.

The red rays of the setting sun embraced Oganda, and she looked like a burning candle in the wilderness.

The people who came to hear her sad song were touched by her beauty. But they all said the same thing: "If it is to save the people, if it is to give us rain, then be not afraid. Your name will forever live among us."

At midnight Oganda was tired and weary. She could walk no more. She sat under a big tree, and having sipped water from her calabash, she rested her head on the tree trunk and slept.

When Oganda woke up in the morning the sun was high in the sky. After walking for many hours, she reached the *tong'*, a strip of land that separated the inhabited part of the country from the sacred place (*kar lamo*). No layman could enter this place and come out alive — only those who had direct contact with the spirits and the Almighty were allowed to enter this holy of holies. But Oganda had to pass through this sacred land on her way to the lake, which she had to reach at sunset.

A large crowd gathered to see her for the last time. Her voice was now hoarse and painful, but there was no need to worry any more. Soon she would not have to sing. The crowd looked at Oganda sympathetically, mumbling words she could not hear. But none of them pleaded for life. As Oganda opened the gate, a child, a young child, broke loose from the crowd, and ran towards her. The child took a small earring from her sweaty hands and gave it to Oganda saying, "When you reach the world of the dead, give this earring to my sister. She died last week. She forgot this ring." Oganda, taken aback by the strange request, took the little ring, and handed her precious water and food to the child. She did not need them now. Oganda did not know whether to laugh or cry. She had heard mourners sending their love to their sweethearts, long dead, but this idea of sending gifts was new to her.

Oganda held her breath as she crossed the barrier to enter the sacred land. She looked appealingly at the crowd, but there was no response. Their minds were too preoccupied with their own survival. Rain was the precious medicine they were longing for, and the sooner Oganda could get to her destination the better.

A strange feeling possessed Oganda as she picked her way in the sacred land. There were strange noises that often startled her, and her first reaction was to take to her heels. But she remembered that she had to fulfil the wish of her people. She was exhausted, but the path was still winding. Then suddenly the path ended on sandy land. The water had retreated miles away from the shore leaving a wide stretch of sand. Beyond this was the vast expanse of water.

Oganda felt afraid. She wanted to picture the size and shape of the monster, but fear would not let her. The society did not talk about it, nor did the crying children who were silenced by the mention of its name. The sun was still up, but it was no longer hot. For a long time Oganda walked ankle-deep in the sand. She was exhausted and longed desperately for her calabash of water. As she moved on, she had a strange feeling that something was following her. Was it the monster? Her hair stood erect, and a cold paralysing feeling ran along her spine. She looked behind, sideways and in front, but there was nothing, except a cloud of dust.

Oganda pulled up and hurried but the feeling did not leave her, and her whole body became saturated with perspiration.

The sun was going down fast and the lake shore seemed to move along with it.

Oganda started to run. She must be at the lake before sunset. As she ran she heard a noise from behind. She looked back sharply, and something resembling a moving bush was frantically running after her. It was about to catch up with her.

Oganda ran with all her strength. She was now determined to throw herself into the water even before sunset. She did not look back, but the creature was upon her. She made an effort to cry out, as in a nightmare, but she could not hear her own voice. The creature caught up with Oganda. In the utter confusion, as Oganda came face to face with the unidentified creature, a strong hand grabbed her. But she fell flat on the sand and fainted.

When the lake breeze brought her back to consciousness, a man was bending over her. ". . . . . !" Oganda opened her mouth to speak, but she had lost her voice. She swallowed a mouthful of water poured into her mouth by the stranger.

"Osinda, Osinda! Please let me die. Let me run, the sun is going down. Let me die, let them have rain." Osinda fondled the glittering chain around Oganda's waist and wiped the tears from her face.

"We must escape quickly to the unknown land," Osinda said urgently. "We must run away from the wrath of the ancestors and the retaliation of the monster."

"But the curse is upon me, Osinda, I am no good to you any more. And moreover the eyes of the ancestors will follow us everywhere and bad luck will befall us. Nor can we escape from the monster."

Oganda broke loose, afraid to escape, but Osinda grabbed her hands again.

"Listen to me, Oganda! Listen! Here are two coats!" He then covered the whole of Oganda's body, except her eyes, with a leafy attire made from the twigs of *Bwombwe*. "These will protect us from the eyes of the ancestors and the wrath of the monster. Now let us run out of here." He held Oganda's hand and they ran from the sacred land, avoiding the path that Oganda had followed.

The bush was thick, and the long grass entangled their feet as they ran. Halfway through the sacred land they stopped and looked back. The sun was almost touching the surface of the water. They were frightened. They continued to run, now faster, to avoid the sinking sun.

"Have faith, Oganda — that thing will not reach us."

When they reached the barrier and looked behind them trembling, only a tip of the sun could be seen above the water's surface.

"It is gone! It is gone!" Oganda wept, hiding her face in her hands.

"Weep not, daughter of the chief. Let us run, let us escape."

There was a bright lightning. They looked up, frightened. Above them black furious clouds started to gather. They began to run. Then the thunder roared, and the rain came down in torrents.

I Am Crying from Thirst

by Alonzo Lopez

*An awareness of the rhythms of nature is
central to Native American culture. Alonzo
Lopez is a member of the Papago tribe of
southern Arizona and northwestern
Mexico—an area that, like Botswana,
consists mainly of desert. This poem
reflects the vital importance of rainwater
in such arid land.*

I am crying from thirst.
I am singing for rain.
I am dancing for rain.
The sky begins to weep,
5   for it sees me
         on the dry, cracked
         earth.

from Waiting for Rain

by Dan Butterworth

Like the villagers of Golema Mmidi, farmers in the U. S. are no strangers to drought. This excerpt is taken from an account of the long, dry summer of 1986, when writer Dan Butterworth lived on a North Carolina farm. Here Butterworth accompanies farmer Archie Clare on his daily circuit to survey the scorched earth.

We crouched in the shade of the truck on a rutted dirt road in Campbell County and surveyed the crop. It looked like death as much as life grew in the fields. As Archie stepped from the truck and crouched, summer tipped its hat. Eighty acres of corn withered as Archie lit his cigarette. Rows of tobacco blistered as he shifted his hat to shade his eyes. As he scratched his chin, all the moisture in three counties dissolved into dust inside melons that hid under leaves wilted to the softness of ashes. Discontentment has a way of easing into thought the way the chalk dust of white heat settles over a stand of pines and smudges the corners of the horizon. It settled on his face as stubble—a finely ground dust of what might have been, a grainy residue of chemicals, curses, and sweat.

First stop of the morning. It was Friday, July 11, and by ten o'clock I had already had too much of the single most constant fact of Archie's work: life in the truck. For most of the year, whenever he shifted the engine into gear his mind had time to idle. But in that morning's ninety-five-degree heat he required all of his energy just to stay awake and hold the wheel, just to distinguish in sounds memories of the self, just to reaffirm that he and the truck were distinct, that he was moving in the world and that the trees, fields, and roads were not a dream. This was the kind of morning that would keep Archie Clare from talking. This was the kind of heat that made even Archie conserve his energy. And what Archie saw left him very little to talk about, even if he had been able to find the words.

Archie saw that there was not a thing to do in that field. In the drought the earth itself appeared to have shriveled up. There was nothing but the inert sand, parched tobacco leaves lofting their fragrance over the soil as they burned slowly in the sun, a whiff of asphalt, a hint of crows, and the memory of a dog in a ditch. Archie climbed back into the truck, poked his ribs for another smoke, stuck it in his mouth and lit it, and turned the key in the ignition. He slowly circled the field, arm stuck out the window, directing the truck by jerking the wheel as he gazed wordlessly at the crop.

On the other side of the road from where the stunted tobacco and field corn wasted away stood his tobacco barns. Next to the road was an old stick barn that Archie no longer used; its aged boards looked pliable as leather. Not more than a hundred feet beyond the stick barn stood two new aluminum bulk barns, set down end to end like two mobile homes. A hundred yards down the road from the barns was an old house with walls the color of dirtied eggshells just pulled from the clutch. When Archie stopped the truck and we climbed out, a pair of turkey vultures circled each other and sank below a line of trees at the back of the property. Archie ignored the tobacco and field corn on the other side of the road and concentrated on the sweet corn that grew in the field behind his tobacco barns—about a quarter acre of Silver Queen between the smaller of the two bulk barns and the old house. We waded over the dead furrow, then walked through the thin green shanks and rough-grained leaves. Archie stopped and ripped open a truncated ear and found it blistered. Squatting between rows of corn I looked up through the green, through so many promises. Looking down I saw black rot and blue mold swelling the tip of an ear at my knee, a tumorous growth bulging from a stalk behind me. Green beetles scurried about exposed roots. . . .

"Overall, things are drying out," Archie said. "Oh, there are cycles—you have your wet years and then your dry years. But by and large the movement all over the country is toward drying out as people clear more land and remove the trees that trap moisture. There is not as much moisture in the earth here as there used to be. You can see that in the swamp. Now the thing about farming is that dry weather will scare you to death, but wet weather will starve you to death. A farmer recalls the wet years a lot better than the dry years. And I'll tell you why. When it's dry, at least he can move about, check the crop, drive into the fields. He doesn't have the sensation of helplessness at least. A farmer's like tobacco—he'll wait for rain too.

"Of course it depends on how you define drought, as well. Dry weather don't make a drought unless your crop fails. What we're experiencing now could go either way. But if it's going to go the wet way it had better hurry up and do it, or it will be too late. As odd as it may sound, most farmers around here will tell you that we have an ideal climate for what we grow. Most farmers wouldn't change the climate a bit. Dry weather gives texture, flavor, and nicotine to the tobacco leaf. Tobacco likes dry weather 'cause it's a weed. Wet tobacco is no good; it produces a wet leaf. . . .

"The question is, what are you going to do about drought? Irrigation is far too expensive unless you have just the right setup and can rig it yourself. Nobody around here will believe in irrigation. There are probably fewer people into irrigation now than twenty-five years ago. The farmers around here who irrigate do it because they picked up the equipment cheap and they have a good source of well water on their land. In California and the desert they have to purchase water by the foot and they run troughs all throughout the fields. Here it's all radial sprinklers. But even with the expense of water out West, irrigation out there makes sense. It don't make a bit of sense where you have a climate that is as unpredictable as ours. In California you can be certain that it won't rain for a month. But here you might could put an inch of water on your crop and the soil will become saturated. But then again it might just rain two inches in the next couple of days and then, boy, you've got problems. What with the soil saturated already and then the extra rain on top of it you could have ruined your crop. So it doesn't pay to irrigate and it doesn't pay not to irrigate. With fifty-fifty odds, and with the memory of years with plenty of moisture, you're not going to find many farmers willing to make the initial investment for an irrigation system. . . .

So what is drought? A degree of brittleness in an oak leaf? Tobacco that won't ripen? Stunted corn? A certain ratio of evapotranspiration per rainfall unit? When some farmers are crushed under drought and five miles away a windfall rain redeems a field of tobacco from three months of crushing heat, when the farmer would rather have baked mud fields to drive on in order to review a crop reduced to parched sticks than have fields so soggy with moisture that he can't get out there to see what's going on, what can make sense in the farmer's world? Drought becomes any breakdown in the circuitry of work. A flaw in the connection between place and place. An unexpected deterioration of energy, as when, with the release of a photon, an electron drops closer to the nucleus. The sapping of the charge from a system. The world as a dead place, an uninhabited body, a landscape devoid of significance. Nature as the brutal machine. The breakdown of conversation.

Crackling Day

by Peter Abrahams

Like Makhaya in When Rain Clouds
Gather, *Peter Abrahams grew up in the
slums of Johannesburg. "Crackling Day"
highlights the everyday degradations
blacks had to suffer under the white South
African regime. What effects might such
routine injustice have on a young person?*

Wednesday was crackling day. On that day the
children of the location made the long trek to Elsburg
siding for the squares of pig's rind that passed for our
daily meat. We collected a double lot of cow dung the
day before; a double lot of moeroga.

I finished my breakfast and washed up. Aunt Liza
was at her washtub in the yard. A misty, sickly sun
was just showing. And on the open veld the frost lay
thick and white on the grass.

"Ready?" Aunt Liza called.

I went out to her. She shook the soapsuds off her
swollen hands and wiped them on her apron. She
lifted the apron and put her hand through the slits of
the many thin cotton dresses she wore. The dress
nearest the skin was the one with the pocket. From
this she pulled a sixpenny piece. She tied it in a knot
in the corner of a bit of coloured cloth and handed it
to me.

"Take care of that. . . .Take the smaller piece of
bread in the bin, but don't eat it till you start back.
You can have a small piece of crackling with it. Only
a small piece, understand?"

"Yes, Aunt Liza."

"All right."

I got the bread and tucked it into the little canvas bag in which I would carry the crackling.

"'Bye, Aunt Liza." I trotted off, one hand in my pocket, feeling the cloth where the money was. I paused at Andries's home.

"Andries!" I danced up and down while I waited. The cold was not so terrible on bare feet if one did not keep still.

Andries came trotting out of his yard. His mother's voice followed; desperate and plaintive:

"I'll skin you if you lose the money!"

"Women!" Andries said bitterly.

I glimpsed the dark, skinny woman at her washtub as we trotted across the veld. Behind and in front of us, other children trotted in twos and threes.

There was a sharp bite to the morning air I sucked in; it stung my nose so that tears came to my eyes; it went down my throat like an icy draught; my nose ran. I tried breathing through my mouth, but this was worse. The cold went through my shirt and shorts; my skin went pimply and chilled; my fingers went numb and began to ache; my feet felt like frozen lumps that did not belong to me, yet jarred and hurt each time I put them down. I began to feel sick and desperate.

"Jesus God in heaven!" Andries cried suddenly.

I looked at him. His eyes were rimmed in red. Tears ran down his cheeks. His face was drawn and purple, a sick look on it.

"Faster," I said.

"Think it'll help?"

I nodded. We went faster. We passed two children, sobbing and moaning as they ran. We were all in the same desperate situation. We were creatures haunted and hounded by the cold. It was a cruel enemy who gave no quarter. And our means of fighting it were pitifully inadequate. In all the mornings and evenings of the winter months, young and old, big and small, were helpless victims of the bitter cold. Only towards noon and in the early afternoon, when the sun sat high in the sky, was there a brief respite. For us children, the cold, especially the morning cold, assumed an awful and malevolent personality. We talked of "it." "It" was a half-human monster with evil thoughts, evil intentions, bent on destroying us. "It" was happiest when we were most miserable. Andries had told me how "it" had, last winter, caught and killed a boy.

Hunger was an enemy too, but one with whom we could come to terms, who had many virtues and values. Hunger gave our pap, moeroga, and crackling a feast-like quality. When it was not with us, we could think and talk kindly about it. Its memory could even give moments of laughter. But the cold of winter was with us all the time. "It" never really eased up. There were only more bearable degrees of "it" at high noon and on mild days. "It" was the real enemy. And on this Wednesday morning, as we ran across the veld, winter was more bitterly, bitingly, freezingly real than ever.

The sun climbed. The frozen earth thawed, leaving the short grass looking wet and weary. Painfully our feet and legs came alive. The aching numbness slowly left our fingers. We ran more slowly in the more bearable cold.

In climbing, the sun lost some of its damp look and seemed a real, if cold, sun. When it was right overhead, we struck the sandy road, which meant we were nearing the siding. None of the others were in sight. Andries and I were alone on the sandy road on the open veld. We slowed down to a brisk walk. We were sufficiently thawed to want to talk.

"How far?" I said.

"A few minutes," he said.

"I've got a piece of bread," I said.

"Me too," he said. "Let's eat it now."

"On the way back," I said. "With a bit of crackling."

"Good idea. . . . Race to the fork."

"All right."

"Go!" he said.

We shot off together, legs working like pistons. He soon pulled away from me. He reached the fork in the road some fifty yards ahead.

"I win!" he shouted gleefully, though his teeth still chattered.

We pitched stones down the road, each trying to pitch farther than the other. I won and wanted to go on doing it. But Andries soon grew weary with pitching. We raced again. Again he won. He wanted another race, but I refused. I wanted pitching, but he refused. So, sulking with each other, we reached the pig farm.

We followed a fenced-off pathway round sprawling white buildings. Everywhere about us was the grunt of pigs. As we passed an open doorway, a huge dog came bounding out, snarling and barking at us. In our terror we forgot it was fenced in, and we streaked away. Surprised, I found myself a good distance ahead of Andries. We looked back and saw a young white woman call the dog to heel.

"Damn Boer dog," Andries said.

"Matter with it?" I asked.

"They teach them to go for us. Never get caught by one. My old man's got a hole in his bottom where a Boer dog got him."

I remembered I had outstripped him.

"I won!" I said.

"Only because you were frightened," he said.

"I still won."

"Scare arse," he jeered.

"Scare arse, yourself!"

"I'll knock you!"

"I'll knock you back!"

A couple of white men came down the path and ended our possible fight. We hurried past them to the distant shed where a queue had already formed. There were grown-ups and children. All the grown-ups and some of the children were from places other than our location.

The line moved slowly. The young white man who served us did it in leisurely fashion, with long pauses for a smoke. Occasionally he turned his back.

At last, after what seemed hours, my turn came. Andries was behind me. I took the sixpenny piece from the square of cloth and offered it to the man.

"Well?" he said.

"Sixpence crackling, please."

Andries nudged me in the back. The man's stare suddenly became cold and hard. Andries whispered into my ear.

"Well?" the man repeated coldly.

"Please *baas*," I said.

"What d'you want?"

"Sixpence crackling, please."

"What?"

Andries dug me in the ribs.

"Sixpence crackling, please, *baas*."

"What?"

"Sixpence crackling, please, *baas*."

"You new here?"

"Yes, *baas*." I looked at his feet, while he stared at me.

At last he took the sixpenny piece from me. I held my bag open while he filled it with crackling from a huge pile on a large canvas sheet on the ground. Turning away, I stole a fleeting glance at his face. His eyes met mine, and there was amused, challenging mockery in them. I waited for Andries at the back of the queue, out of the reach of the white man's mocking eyes.

The cold day was at its mildest as we walked home along the sandy road. I took out my piece of bread and, with a small piece of greasy crackling, still warm, on it, I munched as we went along. We had not yet made our peace, so Andries munched his bread and crackling on the other side of the road.

"Dumb fool!" he mocked at me for not knowing how to address the white man.

"Scare arse!" I shouted back.

Thus, hurling curses at each other, we reached the fork. Andries saw them first and moved over to my side of the road.

"White boys," he said.

There were three of them, two of about our own size and one slightly bigger. They had school bags and were coming towards us up the road from the siding.

"Better run for it," Andries said.

"Why?"

"No, that'll draw them. Let's just walk along, but quickly."

"Why?" I repeated.

"Shut up," he said.

Some of his anxiety touched me. Our own scrap was forgotten. We marched side by side as fast as we could. The white boys saw us and hurried up the road. We passed the fork. Perhaps they would take the turning away from us. We dared not look back.

"Hear them?" Andries asked.

"No." I looked over my shoulder. "They're coming," I said.

"Walk faster," Andries said. "If they come closer, run."

"Hey, *klipkop!*"

"Don't look back," Andries said.

"Hottentot!"

We walked as fast as we could.

"Bloody Kaffir!"

Ahead was a bend in the road. Behind the bend were bushes. Once there, we could run without them knowing it till it was too late.

"Faster," Andries said.

They began pelting us with stones.

"Run when we get to the bushes," Andries said.

The bend and the bushes were near. We would soon be there.

A clear young voice carried to us: "Your fathers are dirty black bastards of baboons!"

"Run!" Andries called.

A violent, unreasoning anger suddenly possessed me. I stopped and turned.

"You're a liar!" I screamed it.

The foremost boy pointed at me. "An ugly black baboon!"

In a fog of rage I went towards him.

"Liar!" I shouted. "My father was better than your father!"

I neared them. The bigger boy stepped between me and the one I was after.

"My father was better than your father! Liar!"

The big boy struck me a mighty clout on the side of the face. I staggered, righted myself, and leaped at the boy who had insulted my father. I struck him on the face, hard. A heavy blow on the back of my head nearly stunned me. I grabbed at the boy in front of me. We went down together.

"Liar!" I said through clenched teeth, hitting him with all my might.

Blows rained on me—on my head, my neck, the side of my face, my mouth—but my enemy was under me and I pounded him fiercely, all the time repeating:

"Liar! Liar! Liar!"

Suddenly stars exploded in my head. Then there was darkness.

I emerged from the darkness to find Andries kneeling beside me.

"God, man! I thought they'd killed you."

I sat up. The white boys were nowhere to be seen. Like Andries, they'd probably thought me dead and run off in panic. The inside of my mouth felt sore and swollen. My nose was tender to the touch. The back of my head ached. A trickle of blood dripped from my nose. I stemmed it with the square of coloured cloth. The greatest damage was to my shirt. It was ripped in many places. I remembered the crackling. I looked anxiously about. It was safe, a little off the road on the grass. I relaxed. I got up and brushed my clothes. I picked up the crackling.

"God, you're dumb!" Andries said. "You're going to get it! Dumb arse!"

I was too depressed to retort. Besides, I knew he was right. I was dumb. I should have run when he told me to.

"Come on," I said.

One of many small groups of children, each child carrying his little bag of crackling, we trod the long road home in the cold winter afternoon.

There was tension in the house that night. When I got back, Aunt Liza had listened to the story in silence. The beating or scolding I expected did not come. But Aunt Liza changed while she listened, became remote and withdrawn. When Uncle Sam came home she told him what had happened. He, too, just looked at me and became more remote and withdrawn than usual. They were waiting for something; their tension reached out to me, and I waited with them, anxious, apprehensive.

The thing we waited for came while we were having

our supper. We heard a trap pull up outside.

"Here it is," Uncle Sam said, and got up.

Aunt Liza leaned back from the table and put her hands in her lap, fingers intertwined, a cold, unseeing look in her eyes.

Before Uncle Sam reached the door, it burst open. A tall, broad, white man strode in. Behind him came the three boys. The one I had attacked had swollen lips and a puffy left eye.

"Evening, *baas*," Uncle Sam murmured.

"That's him," the bigger boy said, pointing at me.

The white man stared till I lowered my eyes.

"Well?" he said.

"He's sorry, *baas*," Uncle Sam said quickly. "I've given him a hiding he won't forget soon. You know how it is, *baas*. He's new here, the child of a relative in Johannesburg, and they don't all know how to behave there. You know how it is in the big towns, *baas*." The plea in Uncle Sam's voice had grown more pronounced as he went on. He turned to me. "Tell the *baas* and young *basies* how sorry you are, Lee."

I looked at Aunt Liza and something in her lifelessness made me stubborn in spite of my fear.

"He insulted my father," I said.

The white man smiled.

"See, Sam, your hiding couldn't have been good."

There was a flicker of life in Aunt Liza's eyes. For a brief moment she saw me, looked at me, warmly, lovingly; then her eyes went dead again.

"He's only a child, *baas*," Uncle Sam murmured.

"You stubborn too, Sam?"

"No, *baas*."

"Good. Then teach him, Sam. If you and he are to live here, you must teach him. Well—?"

"Yes, *baas*."

Uncle Sam went into the other room and returned with a thick leather thong. He wound it once round his hand and advanced on me. The man and the boys leaned against the door, watching. I looked at Aunt Liza's face. Though there was no sign of life or feeling on it, I knew suddenly, instinctively, that she wanted me not to cry.

Bitterly, Uncle Sam said: "You must never lift your hand to a white person. No matter what happens, you must never lift your hand to a white person. . . ."

He lifted the strap and brought it down on my back. I clenched my teeth and stared at Aunt Liza. I did not cry with the first three strokes. Then, suddenly, Aunt Liza went limp. Tears showed in her eyes. The thong came down on my back again and again. I screamed and begged for mercy. I grovelled at Uncle Sam's feet, begging him to stop, promising never to lift my hand to any white person. . . .

At last the white man's voice said: "All right, Sam."

Uncle Sam stopped. I lay whimpering on the floor. Aunt Liza sat like one in a trance.

"Is he still stubborn, Sam?"

"Tell the *baas* and *basies* you are sorry."

"I'm sorry," I said.

"Bet his father is one of those who believe in equality."

"His father is dead," Aunt Liza said.

"Good night, Sam."

"Good night, *baas*. Sorry about this."

"All right, Sam." He opened the door. The boys went out first, then he followed. "Good night, Liza."

Aunt Liza did not answer. The door shut behind the white folk, and soon we heard their trap moving away. Uncle Sam flung the thong viciously against the door, slumped down on the bench, folded his arms on the table, and buried his head on his arms. Aunt Liza moved away from him, sat down on the floor beside me, and lifted me into her large lap. She sat rocking my body. Uncle Sam began to sob softly. After some time he raised his head and looked at us.

"Explain to the child, Liza," he said.

"You explain," Aunt Liza said bitterly. "You are the man. You did the beating. You are the head of the family. This is a man's world. You do the explaining."

"Please, Liza."

"You should be happy. The whites are satisfied. We can go on now."

With me in her arms, Aunt Liza got up. She carried me into the other room. The food on the table remained half-eaten. She laid me on the bed on my stomach, smeared fat on my back, then covered me with the blankets. She undressed and got into bed beside me. She cuddled me close, warmed me with her own body. With her big hand on my cheek, she rocked me, first to silence, then to sleep.

For the only time during my stay there, I slept on a bed in Elsburg.

When I woke next morning, Uncle Sam had gone. Aunt Liza only once referred to the beating he had given me. It was in the late afternoon, when I returned with the day's cow dung.

"It hurt him," she said. "You'll understand one day."

That night Uncle Sam brought me an orange, a bag of boiled sweets, and a dirty old picture book. He smiled as he gave them to me, rather anxiously. When I smiled back at him, he seemed to relax. He put his hand on my head, started to say something, then changed his mind and took his seat by the fire.

Aunt Liza looked up from the floor, where she dished out the food.

"It's all right, old man," she murmured.

"One day . . ." Uncle Sam said.

"It's all right," Aunt Liza repeated insistently.

Some Monday for Sure

by Nadine Gordimer

Is violence ever justified? Makhaya in
When Rain Clouds Gather *believes there*
are times when it is. The characters in the
following story live under the same
oppressive regime that Makhaya fights
and flees—white South Africa. Because of
his job working with explosives, Josias and
his brother-in-law Willie find themselves
involved in a dangerous and desperate
plan.

My sister's husband, Josias, used to work on the
railways but then he got this job where they make
dynamite for the mines. He was the one who sits out
on that little iron seat clamped to the back of the big
red truck, with a red flag in his hand. The idea is that
if you drive up too near the truck or look as if you're
going to crash into it, he waves the flag to warn you
off. You've seen those trucks often on the Main Reef
Road between Johannesburg and the mining towns—
they carry the stuff and have DANGER—
EXPLOSIVES painted on them. The man sits there,
with an iron chain looped across his little seat to keep
him from being thrown into the road, and he clutches
his flag like a kid with a balloon. That's how Josias
was, too. Of course, if you didn't take any notice of
the warning and went on and crashed into the truck,
he would be the first to be blown to high heaven and

hell, but he always just sits there, this chap, as if he has no idea when he was born or that he might not die on a bed an old man of eighty. As if the dust in his eyes and the racket of the truck are going to last forever.

My sister knew she had a good man but she never said anything about being afraid of this job. She only grumbled in winter, when he was stuck out there in the cold and used to get a cough (she's a nurse), and on those times in summer when it rained all day and she said he would land up with rheumatism, crippled, and then who would give him work? The dynamite people? I don't think it ever came into her head that any day, every day, he could be blown up instead of coming home in the evening. Anyway, you wouldn't have thought so by the way she took it when he told us what it was he was going to have to do.

I was working down at a garage in town, that time, at the petrol pumps, and I was eating before he came in because I was on night shift. Emma had the water ready for him and he had a wash without saying much, as usual, but then he didn't speak when they sat down to eat, either, and when his fingers went into the mealie meal he seemed to forget what it was he was holding and not to be able to shape it into a mouthful. Emma must have thought he felt too dry to eat, because she got up and brought him a jam tin of the beer she had made for Saturday. He drank it and then sat back and looked from her to me, but she said, "Why don't you eat?" and he began to, slowly. She said, "What's the matter with you?" He got up and yawned and yawned, showing those brown chipped teeth that remind me of the big ape at the Johannesburg zoo that I saw once when I went with the school. He went into the other room of the house, where he and Emma slept, and he came back with his pipe. He filled it carefully, the way a poor man does; I saw, as soon as I went to work at the filling station, how the white men fill their pipes, stuffing the tobacco in, picking out any bits they don't like the look of, shoving the tin half shut back into the glove box of the car. "I'm going down to Sela's place," said Emma. "I can go with Willie on his way to work if you don't want to come."

"No. Not tonight. You stay here." Josias always speaks like this, the short words of a schoolmaster or a boss-boy, but if you hear the way he says them, you know he is not really ordering you around at all, he is only asking you.

"No, I told her I'm coming," Emma said, in the voice of a woman having her own way in a little thing.

"Tomorrow." Josias began to yawn again, looking at us with wet eyes. "Go to bed," Emma said. "I won't be late."

"No, no, I want to . . ." He blew a sigh. "When he's gone, man—" He moved his pipe at me. "I'll tell you later."

Emma laughed. "What can you tell that Willie can't hear." I've lived with them ever since they were married. Emma always was the one who looked after me, even before, when I was a little kid. It was true that whatever happened to us happened to us together. He looked at me; I suppose he saw that I was a man, now: I was in my blue overalls with *Shell* on the pocket and everything.

He said, "They want me to do something . . . a job with the truck."

Josias used to turn out regularly to political meetings and he took part in a few protests before everything went underground, but he had never been more than one of the crowd. We had Mandela and the rest of the leaders, cut out of the paper, hanging on the wall, but he had never known, personally, any of them. Of course there were his friends Ndhlovu and Seb Masinde who said they had gone underground and who occasionally came late at night for a meal or slept in my bed for a few hours.

"They want to stop the truck on the road—"

"Stop it?" Emma was like somebody stepping into cold dark water; with every word that was said she went deeper. "But how can you do it—when? Where will they do it?" She was wild, as if she must go out and prevent it all happening right then.

I felt that cold water of Emma's rising round the belly because Emma and I often had the same feelings, but I caught also, in Josias's not looking at me, a signal Emma couldn't know. Something in me jumped at it like catching a swinging rope. "They want the stuff inside . . . ?"

Nobody said anything.

I said, "What a lot of big bangs you could make with that, man," and then shut up before Josias needed to tell me to.

"So what're you going to do?" Emma's mouth stayed open after she had spoken, the lips pulled back.

"They'll tell me everything. I just have to give them the best place on the road—that'll be the Free State road, the others're too busy . . . and . . . the time when we pass. . . ."

"You'll be dead." Emma's head was shuddering and her whole body shook; I've never seen anybody give up like that. He was dead already, she saw it with her eyes and she was kicking and screaming without knowing how to show it to him. She looked like she wanted to kill Josias herself, for being dead. "That'll be the finish, for sure. He's got a gun, the white man in front, hasn't he, you told me. And the one with him? They'll kill you. You'll go to prison. They'll take you to Pretoria jail and hang you by the rope. . . . Yes, he's got the gun, you told me, didn't you—many times you told me—"

"The others've got guns too. How d'you think they

can hold us up? They've got guns and they'll come all round him. It's all worked out—"

"The one in front will shoot you, I know it, don't tell me, I know what I say. . . ." Emma went up and down and around till I thought she would push the walls down—they wouldn't have needed much pushing, in that house in Tembekile Location—and I was scared of her. I don't mean for what she would do to me if I got in her way, or to Josias, but for what might happen to her: something like taking a fit or screaming that none of us would be able to forget.

I don't think Josias was sure about doing the job before but he wanted to do it now. "No shooting. Nobody will shoot me. Nobody will know that I know anything. Nobody will know I tell them anything. I'm held up just the same like the others! Same as the white man in front! Who can shoot me? They can shoot me for that?"

"Someone else can go, I don't want it, do you hear? You will stay at home, I will say you are sick. . . . You will be killed, they will shoot you. . . . Josias, I'm telling you, I don't want . . . I won't . . ."

I was waiting my chance to speak, all the time, and I felt Josias was waiting to talk to someone who had caught the signal. I said quickly, while she went on and on, "But even on that road there are some cars?"

"Roadblocks," he said, looking at the floor. "They've got the signs, the ones you see when a road's being dug up, and there'll be some men with picks. After the truck goes through they'll block the road so that any other cars turn off onto the old road there by Kalmansdrif. The same thing on the other side, two miles on. There where the farm road goes down to Nek Halt."

"Hell, man! Did you have to pick what part of the road?"

"I know it like this yard. Don't I?"

Emma stood there, between the two of us, while we discussed the whole business. We didn't have to worry about anyone hearing, not only because Emma kept the window wired up in that kitchen, but also because the yard the house was in was a real Tembekile Location one, full of babies yelling and people shouting, night and day, not to mention the transistors playing in the houses all round. Emma was looking at us all the time and out of the corner of my eye I could see her big front going up and down fast in the neck of her dress.

". . . so they're going to tie you up as well as the others?"

He drew on his pipe to answer me.

We thought for a moment and then grinned at each other; it was the first time for Josias, that whole evening.

Emma began collecting the dishes under our noses. She dragged the tin bath of hot water from the stove and washed up. "I said I'm taking my off on Wednesday. I suppose this is going to be next week." Suddenly, yet talking as if carrying on where she let up, she was quite different.

"I don't know."

"Well, I have to know because I suppose I must be at home."

"What must you be at home for?" said Josias.

"If the police come I don't want them talking to *him*," she said, looking at us both without wanting to see us.

"The police—" said Josias, and jerked his head to send them running, while I laughed, to show her.

"And I want to know what I must say."

"What must you say? Why? They can get my statement from me when they find us tied up. In the night I'll be back here myself."

"Oh yes," she said, scraping the mealie meal he

hadn't eaten back into the pot. She did everything as usual; she wanted to show us nothing was going to wait because of this big thing, she must wash the dishes and put ash on the fire. "You'll be back, oh yes.—Are you going to sit here all night, Willie?—Oh yes, you'll be back."

And then, I think, for a moment Josias saw himself dead, too; he didn't answer when I took my cap and said, so long, from the door.

I knew it must be a Monday. I notice that women quite often don't remember ordinary things like this, I don't know what they think about—for instance, Emma didn't catch on that it must be Monday, next Monday or the one after, some Monday for sure, because Monday was the day that we knew Josias went with the truck to the Free State mines. It was Friday when he told us and all day Saturday I had a terrible feeling that it was going to be *that* Monday, and it would be all over before I could—what? I didn't know, man. I felt I must at least see where it was going to happen. Sunday I was off work and I took my bicycle and rode into town before there was even anybody in the streets and went to the big station and found that although there wasn't a train on Sundays that would take me all the way, I could get one that would take me about thirty miles. I had to pay to put the bike in the luggage van as well as for my ticket, but I'd got my wages on Friday. I got off at the nearest halt to Kalmansdrif and then I asked people along the road the best way. It was a long ride, more than two hours. I came out on the main road from the sand road just at the turnoff Josias had told me about. It was just like he said: a tin sign KALMANSDRIF pointing down the road I'd come from. And the nice blue tarred road, smooth, straight ahead: was I glad to get onto it! I hadn't taken much notice of the country so far, while I was sweating along, but from then on I woke up and saw everything. I've only got to think about it to see it again now. The veld is flat round about there, it was the end of winter, so the grass was dry. Quite far away and very far apart, there was a hill, and then another, sticking up in the middle of nothing, pink colour, and with its point cut off like the neck of a bottle. Ride and ride, these hills never got any nearer and there were none beside the road. It all looked empty and the sky much bigger than the ground, but there were some people there. It's funny you don't notice them like you do in town. All our people, of course; there were barbed-wire fences, so it must have been white farmers' land, but they've got the water and their houses are far off the road and you can usually see them only by the big dark trees that hide them. Our people had mud houses and there would be three or four in the same place made bare by goats and people's feet. Often the huts were near a kind of crack in the ground, where the little kids played and where, I suppose, in summer, there was water. Even now the women were managing to do washing in some places. I saw children run to the road to jig about and stamp when cars passed, but the men and women took no interest in what was up there. It was funny to think that I was just like them, now, men and women who are always busy inside themselves with jobs, plans, thinking about how to get money or how to talk to someone about something important, instead of like the children, as I used to be only a few years ago, taking in each small thing around them as it happens.

Still, there were people living pretty near the road. What would they do if they saw the dynamite truck held up and a fight going on? (I couldn't think of it, then, in any other way except like I'd seen hold-ups in Westerns, although I've seen plenty of fighting, all my life, among the Location gangs and drunks—I was ashamed not to be able to forget those kid-stuff Westerns at a time like this.) Would they go running away to the white farmer? Would somebody jump on a bike and go for the police? Or if there was no bike, what about a horse? I saw someone riding a horse.

I rode slowly to the next turn-off, the one where a farm road goes down to Nek Halt. There it was, just like Josias said. Here was where the other roadblock would be. But when he spoke about it there was nothing in between! No people, no houses, no flat veld with hills on it! It had been just one of those things grown-ups see worked out in their heads: while all the time, here it was, a real place where people had cooking fires, I could hear a herdboy yelling at a dirty bundle of sheep, a big bird I've never seen in town balanced on the barbed-wire fence right in front of me. . . . I got off my bike and it flew away.

I sat a minute on the side of the road. I'd had a cold drink in an Indian shop in the dorp where I'd got off the train, but I was dry again inside my mouth, while plenty of water came out of my skin, I can tell you. I rode back down the road looking for the exact place I would choose if I were Josias. There was a stretch where there was only one kraal consisting of two houses, and that quite a way back from the road. Also there was a dip where the road went over a donga. Old stumps of trees and nothing but cows' business down there; men could hide. I got off again and had a good look round.

But I wondered about the people, up top. I don't know why it was, I wanted to know about those people just as though I was going to have to go and live with them, or something. I left the bike down in the donga and crossed the road behind a Cadillac going so fast the air smacked together after it, and I began to trek over the veld to the houses. I know most of our people live like this, in the veld, but I'd never been into houses like that before. I was born in some Location (I don't know which one, I must ask Emma one day) and Emma and I lived in Goughville Location with our grandmother. Our mother worked in town and she used to come and see us sometimes, but we never saw our father and Emma thinks that perhaps we didn't have the same father, because she remembers a man before I was born, and after I was born she didn't see him again. I don't really remember anyone, from when I was a little kid, except Emma. Emma dragging me along so fast my arm almost came off my body, because we had nearly been caught by the Indian while stealing peaches from his lorry: we did that every day.

We lived in one room with our grandmother but it was a tin house with a number and later on there was a streetlight at the corner. These houses I was coming to had a pattern all over them marked into the mud they were built of. There was a mound of dried cows' business, as tall as I was, stacked up in a pattern, too. And then the usual junk our people have, just like in the Location: old tins, broken things collected in white people's rubbish heaps. The fowls ran sideways from my feet and two old men let their talking die away into ahas and ehês as I came up. I greeted them the right way to greet old men and they nodded and went on ehêing and ahaing to show that they had been greeted properly. One of them had very clean ragged trousers tied with string and sat on the ground, but the other, sitting on a bucket seat that must have been taken from some scrapyard car, was dressed in a way I've never seen—from the old days, I suppose. He wore a black suit with very wide trousers, laced boots, a stiff white collar and black tie, and on top of it all, a broken old hat. It was Sunday, of course, so I suppose he was all dressed up. I've heard that these people who work for farmers wear sacks most of the time. The old ones didn't ask me what I wanted there. They just peered at me with their eyes gone the colour of soapy water because they were so old. And I didn't know what to say because I hadn't thought what I was going to say, I'd just walked. Then a little kid slipped out of the dark doorway quick as a cockroach. I thought perhaps everyone else was out because it was Sunday but then a voice called from inside the other house, and when the child didn't answer, called again, and a woman came to the doorway.

I said my bicycle had a puncture and could I have some water.

She said something into the house and in a minute a girl, about fifteen she must've been, edged past her carrying a paraffin tin and went off to fetch water. Like all the girls that age, she never looked at you. Her body shook under an ugly old dress and she almost hobbled in her hurry to get away. Her head was tied up in a rag-doek right down to the eyes the way old-fashioned people do, otherwise she would have been quite pretty, like any other girl. When she had gone a little way the kid went pumping after her, panting, yelling, opening his skinny legs wide as scissors over stones and antheaps, and then he caught up with her and you could see that right away she was quite different, I knew how it was, she yelled at him, you heard her laughter as she chased him with the tin, whirled around from out of his clutching hands, struggled with him; they were together like Emma and I used to be when we got away from the old lady, and from the school, and everybody. And Emma was also one of our girls who have the big strong comfortable bodies of mothers even when they're still kids, maybe it comes from always lugging the smaller one round on their backs.

A man came out of the house behind the woman and was friendly. His hair had the dusty look of someone who's been sleeping off drink. In fact, he was still a bit heavy with it.

"You coming from Jo'burg?"

But I wasn't going to be caught out being careless at all, Josias could count on me for that.

"Vereeniging."

He thought there was something funny there—nobody dresses like a Jo'burger, you could always spot us a mile off—but he was too full to follow it up.

He stood stretching his sticky eyelids open and then he fastened on me the way some people will do: "Can't you get me work there where you are?"

"What kind of work?"

He waved a hand describing me. "You got a good work."

"'Sall right."

"Where you working now?"

"Garden boy."

He tittered, "Look like you work in town," shook his head.

I was surprised to find the woman handing me a tin of beer, and I squatted on the ground to drink it. It's mad to say that a mud house can be pretty, but those patterns made in the mud looked nice. They must have been done with a sharp stone or stick when the mud was smooth and wet, the shapes of things like big leaves and moons filled in with lines that went all one way in this shape, another way in that, so that as you looked at the walls in the sun, some shapes were dark and some were light, and if you moved, the light ones went dark and the dark ones got light instead. The girl came back with the heavy tin of water on her head making her neck thick. I washed out the jam tin I'd had the beer in and filled it with water. When I thanked them, the old men stirred and ahaed and ehêed again. The man made as if to walk a bit with me, but I was lucky, he didn't go more than a few yards. "No good," he said. "Every morning, five o'clock, and the pay—very small."

How I would have hated to be him, a man already married and with big children, working all his life in the fields wearing sacks. When you think like this about someone he seems something you could never possibly be, as if it's his fault, and not just the chance of where he happened to be born. At the same time I had a crazy feeling I wanted to tell him something wonderful, something he'd never dreamed could happen, something he'd fall on his knees and thank me for. I wanted to say, "Soon you'll be the farmer yourself and you'll have shoes like me and your girl will get water from your windmill. Because on Monday, or another Monday, the truck will stop down there and all the stuff will be taken away and they—Josias, me; even you, yes—we'll win forever." But instead all I said was, "Who did that on your house?" He didn't understand and I made a drawing in the air with my hand. "The women," he said, not interested.

Down in the donga I sat a while and then threw away the tin and rode off without looking up again to where the kraal was.

It wasn't that Monday. Emma and Josias go to bed very early and of course they were asleep by the time I got home late on Sunday night—Emma thought I'd been with the boys I used to go around with at weekends. But Josias got up at half past four every morning, then, because it was a long way from the Location to where the dynamite factory was, and although I didn't usually even hear him making the fire in the kitchen which was also where I was sleeping, that morning I was awake the moment he got out of bed next door. When he came into the kitchen I was sitting up in my blankets and I whispered loudly, "I went there yesterday. I saw the turn-off and everything. Down there by the donga, ay? Is that the place?"

He looked at me, a bit dazed. He nodded. Then: "Wha'd' you mean you went there?"

"I could see that's the only good place. I went up to the houses, too, just to see . . . the people are all right. Not many. When it's not Sunday there may be nobody there but the old man—there were two, I think one was just a visitor. The man and the women will be over in the fields somewhere, and that must be quite far, because you can't see the mealies from the road. . . ." I could feel myself being listened to carefully, getting in with him (and if with him, with *them*) while I was talking, and I knew exactly what I was saying, absolutely clearly, just as I would know exactly what I was doing. He began to question me; but like I was an older man or a clever one; he didn't know what to say. He drank his tea while I told him all about it. He was thinking. Just before he left he said, "I shouldn't've told you."

I ran after him, outside, into the yard. It was still dark. I blurted in the same whisper we'd been using, "Not today, is it?" I couldn't see his face properly but I knew he didn't know whether to answer or not. "Not today." I was so happy I couldn't go to sleep again.

In the evening Josias managed to make some excuse to come out with me alone for a bit. He said, "I told them you were a hundred-per-cent. It's just the same as if I know." "Of course, no difference. I just haven't had much of a chance to do anything . . ." I didn't carry on: ". . . because I was too young"; we didn't want to bring Emma into it. And anyway, no one but a real kid is too young any more. Look at the boys who are up for sabotage. I said, "Have they got them all?"

He hunched his shoulders.

"I mean, even the ones for the picks and spades . . . ?"

He wouldn't say anything, but I knew I could ask. "Oh, boetie, man, even just to keep a lookout, there on the road. . . ."

I know he didn't want it but once they knew I knew, and that I'd been there and everything, they were keen to use me. At least that's what I think. I never went to any meetings or anything where it was planned, and beforehand I only met the two others who were with me at the turn-off in the end, and we were told exactly what we had to do by Seb Masinde. Of course, neither of us said a word to Emma. The Monday that we did it was three weeks later and I can tell you, although a lot's happened to me since then, I'll never forget the moment when we flagged the truck through with Josias sitting there on the back in his little seat. Josias! I wanted to laugh and shout there in the veld; I didn't feel scared—what was there to be scared of, he'd been sitting on a load of dynamite every day of his life for years now, so what's the odds. We had one of those tins of fire and a bucket of tar and the real ROAD CLOSED signs from the PWD and everything went smooth at our end. It was at the Nek Halt end that the trouble started when one of these AA patrol bikes had to come along (Josias says it was something new, they'd never met a patrol on that road that time of day, before) and get suspicious about the block there. In the meantime the truck was stopped all right but someone was shot and Josias tried to get the gun from the white man up in front of the truck and there was a hell of a fight and they had to make a getaway with the stuff in a car and van back through our block, instead of taking over the truck and driving it to a hiding place to offload. More than half the stuff had to be left behind in the truck. Still, they got clean away with what they did get and it was never found by the police. Whenever I read in the papers here that something's been blown up back at home, I wonder if it's still one of our bangs. Two of our people got picked up right away and some more later and the whole thing was all over the papers with speeches by the chief of Special Branch about a master plot and everything. But Josias got away okay. We three chaps at the roadblock just ran into the veld to where there were bikes hidden. We went to a place we'd been told in Rustenburg district for a week and then we were told to get over to Bechuanaland. It wasn't so bad; we had no money but around Rustenburg it was easy to pinch pawpaws and oranges off the farms. . . . Oh, I sent a message to Emma that I was all right; and at that time it didn't seem true that I couldn't go home again.

But in Bechuanaland it was different. We had no money, and you don't find food on trees in that dry place. They said they would send us money; it didn't come. But Josias was there too, and we stuck together; people hid us and we kept going. Planes arrived and took away the big shots and the white refugees but although we were told we'd go too, it never came off. We had no money to pay for ourselves. There were plenty others like us in the beginning. At last we just walked, right up Bechuanaland and through Northern Rhodesia to Mbeya, that's over the border in Tanganyika, where we were headed for. A long walk; took Josias and me months. We met up with a chap who'd been given a bit of money and from there sometimes we went by bus. No one asks questions when you're nobody special and you walk, like all the other African people themselves, or take the buses, that the whites never use; it's only if you've got the money for cars or to arrive at the airports that all these things happen that you read about: getting sent back over the border, refused permits, and so on. So we got here, to Tanganyika at last, down to this town of Dar es Salaam where we'd been told we'd be going.

There's a refugee camp here and they give you a shilling or two a day until you get work. But it's out of town, for one thing, and we soon left there and found a room down in the native town. There are some nice buildings, of course, in the real town— nothing like Johannesburg or Durban, though—and that used to be the white town, the whites who are left still live there, but the Africans with big jobs in the government and so on live there too. Some of our leaders who are refugees like us live in these houses and have big cars; everyone knows they're important men, here, not like at home where if you're black you're just rubbish for the Locations. The people down where we lived are very poor and it's hard to get work because they haven't got enough work for themselves, but I've got my standard seven and I managed to get a small job as a clerk. Josias never found steady work. But that didn't matter so much because the big thing was that Emma was able to come to join us after five months, and she and I earn the money. She's a nurse, you see, and Africanization started in the hospitals and the government was short of nurses. So Emma got the chance to come up with a party of them sent for specially from South Africa and Rhodesia. We were very lucky because it's impossible for people to get their families up here. She came in a plane paid for by the government, and she and the other girls had their photograph taken for the newspaper as they got off at the airport. That day she came we took her to the beach, where everyone can bathe, no restrictions, and for a cool drink in one of the hotels (she'd never been in a hotel before), and we walked up and down the road along the bay where everyone walks and where you can see the ships coming in and going out so near that the men out there wave to you. Whenever we bumped into anyone else from home they would stop and ask her about home, and how everything was. Josias and I couldn't stop grinning to hear us all, in the middle of Dar, talking away in our language about the things we know. That day it was like it had happened already: the time when we are home again and everything is our way.

Well, that's nearly three years ago, since Emma came. Josias has been sent away now and there's only Emma and me. That was always the idea, to send us away for training. Some go to Ethiopia and some go to Algeria and all over the show and by the time they come back there won't be anything Verwoerd's men know in the way of handling guns and so on that they won't know better. That's for a start. I'm supposed to go too, but some of us have been waiting a long time. In the meantime I go to work and I walk about this place in the evenings and I buy myself a glass of beer in a bar when I've got money. Emma and I have still got the flat we had before Josias left and two nurses from the hospital pay us for the other bedroom. Emma still works at the hospital but I don't know how much longer. Most days now since Josias's gone she wants me to walk up to fetch her from the hospital when she comes off duty, and when I get under the trees on the drive I see her staring out looking for me as if I'll never turn up ever again. Every day it's like that. When I come up she smiles and looks like she used to for a minute but by the time we're ten yards on the road she's shaking and shaking her head until the tears come, and saying over and over, "A person can't stand it, a person can't stand it." She said right from the beginning that the hospitals here are not like the hospitals at home, where the nurses have to know their job. She's got a whole ward in her charge and now she says they're worse and worse and she can't trust anyone to do anything for her. And the staff don't like having strangers working with them anyway. She tells me every day like she's telling me for the first time. Of course it's true that some of the people don't like us being here. You know how it is, people haven't got enough jobs to go around, themselves. But I don't take much notice; I'll be sent off one of these days and until then I've got to eat and that's that.

The flat is nice with a real bathroom and we are paying off the table and six chairs she liked so much, but when we walk in, her face is terrible. She keeps saying the place will never be straight. At home there was only a tap in the yard for all the houses but she never said it there. She doesn't sit down for more than a minute without getting up at once again, but you can't get her to go out, even on these evenings when it's so hot you can't breathe. I go down to the market to buy the food now, she says she can't stand it. When I asked why—because at the beginning she used to like the market, where you can pick a live fowl for yourself, quite cheap—she said those little rotten tomatoes they grow here, and dirty people all shouting and she can't understand. She doesn't sleep, half the time, at night, either, and lately she wakes me up. It happened only last night. She was standing there in the dark and she said, "I felt bad." I said, "I'll make you some tea," though what good could tea do. "There must be something the matter with me," she says. "I must go to the doctor tomorrow."

"Is it pains again, or what?"

She shakes her head slowly, over and over, and I know she's going to cry again. "A place where there's no one. I get up and look out the window and it's just like I'm not awake. And every day, every day. I can't ever wake up and be out of it. I always see this town."

Of course it's hard for her. I've picked up Swahili and I can get around all right; I mean I can always talk to anyone if I feel like it, but she hasn't learnt more than *ahsante*—she could've picked it up just as easily, but she *can't*, if you know what I mean. It's just a noise to her, like dogs barking or those black crows in the palm trees. When anyone does come here to see her—someone else from home, usually, or perhaps I bring the Rhodesian who works where I do—she only sits there and whatever anyone talks about she doesn't listen until she can sigh and say, "Heavy, heavy. Yes, for a woman alone. No friends, nobody. For a woman alone, I can tell you."

Last night I said to her, "It would be worse if you were at home, you wouldn't have seen Josias or me for a long time."

But she said, "Yes, it would be bad. Sela and everybody. And the old crowd at the hospital—but just the same, it would be bad. D'you remember how we used to go right into town on my Saturday off? The people—ay! Even when you were twelve you used to be scared you'd lose me."

"I wasn't scared, you were the one was scared to get run over sometimes." But in the Location when we stole fruit, and sweets from the shops, Emma could always grab me out of the way of trouble, Emma always saved me. The same Emma. And yet it's not the same. And what could I do for her?

I suppose she wants to be back there now. But still she wouldn't be the same. I don't often get the feeling she knows what I'm thinking about, any more, or that I know what she's thinking, but she said, "You and he go off, you come back or perhaps you don't come back, you know what you must do. But for a woman? What shall I do there in my life? What shall I do here? What time is this for a woman?"

It's hard for her. Emma. She'll say all that often now, I know. She tells me everything so many times. Well, I don't mind it when I fetch her from the hospital and I don't mind going to the market. But straight after we've eaten, now, in the evenings, I let her go through it once and then I'm off. To walk in the streets when it gets a bit cooler in the dark. I don't know why it is, but I'm thinking so bloody hard about getting out there in the streets that I push down my food as fast as I can without her noticing. I'm so keen to get going I feel queer, kind of tight and excited. Just until I can get out and not hear. I wouldn't even mind skipping the meal. In the streets in the evening everyone is out. On the grass along the bay the fat Indians in their white suits with their wives in those fancy coloured clothes. Men and their girls holding hands. Old watchmen like beggars, sleeping in the doorways of the shut shops. Up and down people walk, walk, just sliding one foot after the other because now and then, like somebody lifting a blanket, there's air from the sea. She should come out for a bit of air in the evening, man. It's an old, old place this, they say. Not the buildings, I mean; but the place. They say ships were coming here before even a place like London was a town. She thought the bay was so nice, that first day. The lights from the ships run all over the water and the palms show up a long time even after it gets dark. There's a smell I've smelled ever since we've been here—three years! I don't mean the smells in the native town; a special warm night-smell. You can even smell it at three in the morning. I've smelled it when I was standing about with Emma, by the window; it's as hot in the middle of the night here as it is in the middle of the day, at home—funny, when you look at the stars and the dark. Well, I'll be going off soon. It can't be long now. Now that Josias is gone. You've just got to wait your time; they haven't forgotten about you. Dar es Salaam. Dar. Sometimes I walk with another chap from home, he says some things, makes you laugh! He says the old watchmen who sleep in the doorways get their wives to come there with them. Well, I haven't seen it. He says we're definitely going with the next lot. Dar es Salaam. Dar. One day I suppose I'll remember it and tell my wife I stayed three years there, once. I walk and walk, along the bay, past the shops and hotels and the German church and the big bank, and through the mud streets between old shacks and stalls. It's dark there and full of other walking shapes as I wander past light coming from the cracks in the walls, where the people are in their homes.

I Am Not One of Those Who Left the Land

by Anna Akhmatova, translated by
Stanley Kunitz with Max Hayward

*Was Mahkaya right to go into exile from
his native South Africa? What alternative
did he face? In this poem, written shortly
after a civil war in Russia (1918–1920),
Anna Akhmatova expresses her attitude
toward those who have deserted her
country in times of strife.*

I am not one of those who left the land
to the mercy of its enemies.
Their flattery leaves me cold,
my songs are not for them to praise.

5   But I pity the exile's lot.
Like a felon, like a man half-dead,
dark is your path, wanderer;
wormwood infects your foreign bread.

But here, in the murk of conflagration,
10   where scarcely a friend is left to know,
we, the survivors, do not flinch
from anything, not from a single blow.

Surely the reckoning will be made
after the passing of this cloud.
15   We are the people without tears,
straighter than you . . . more proud . . .

Spring Sowing

by Liam O'Flaherty

*The fields of Ireland are very different
from the land around Golema Mmidi. But
some aspects of working the land are
shared the world over. As you read the
following story, think about the similarities
and differences between Makhaya and
Paulina's world and that of this Irish
farming couple.*

It was still dark when Martin Delaney and his wife
Mary got up. Martin stood in his shirt by the window
a long time looking out, rubbing his eyes and
yawning, while Mary raked out the live coals that had
lain hidden in the ashes on the hearth all night.
Outside, cocks were crowing and a white streak was
rising from the ground, as it were, and beginning to
scatter the darkness. It was a February morning, dry,
cold and starry.

The couple sat down to their breakfast of tea, bread
and butter, in silence. They had only been married the
previous autumn and it was hateful leaving a warm bed
at such an early hour. They both felt in a bad humor
and ate, wrapped in their thoughts. Martin, with his
brown hair and eyes, his freckled face and his little fair
moustache, looked too young to be married, and his
wife looked hardly more than a girl, red-cheeked and
blue-eyed, her black hair piled at the rear of her head
with a large comb gleaming in the middle of the pile,
Spanish fashion. They were both dressed in rough
homespuns, and both wore the loose white frieze shirt
that Inverara peasants use for work in the fields.

They ate in silence, sleepy and bad-humoured and yet on fire with excitement, for it was the first day of their first spring sowing as man and wife. And each felt the glamour of that day on which they were to open up the earth together and plant seeds in it. So they sat in silence and bad humour, for somehow the imminence of an event that had been long expected, loved, feared and prepared for made them dejected. Mary, with her shrewd woman's mind, munched her bread and butter and thought of . . . Oh, what didn't she think of? Of as many things as there are in life does a woman think in the first joy and anxiety of her mating. But Martin's mind was fixed on one thought. Would he be able to prove himself a man worthy of being the head of a family by doing his spring sowing well?

In the barn after breakfast, when they were getting the potato seeds and the line for measuring the ground and the spade, a cross word or two passed between them, and when Martin fell over a basket in the half-darkness of the barn, he swore and said that a man would be better off dead than . . . But before he could finish whatever he was going to say, Mary had her arms around his waist and her face to his. "Martin," she said, "let us not begin this day cross with one another." And there was a tremor in her voice. And somehow, as they embraced and Martin kept mumbling in his awkward peasant's voice, "pulse of my heart, treasure of my life," and such traditional phrases, all their irritation and sleepiness left them. And they stood there embracing until at last Martin pushed her from him with pretended roughness and said: "Come, come, girl, it will be sunset before we begin at this rate."

Still, as they walked silently in their rawhide shoes through the little hamlet, there was not a soul about. Lights were glimmering in the windows of a few cabins. The sky had a big gray crack in it in the east, as if it were going to burst in order to give birth to the sun. Birds were singing somewhere at a distance. Martin and Mary rested their baskets of seeds on a fence outside the village and Martin whispered to Mary proudly: "We are first, Mary." And they both looked back at the little cluster of cabins that was the centre of their world, with throbbing hearts. For the joy of spring had now taken complete hold of them.

They reached the little field where they were to sow. It was a little triangular patch of ground under an ivy-covered limestone hill. The little field had been manured with seaweed some weeks before, and the weeds had rotted and whitened on the grass. And there was a big red heap of fresh seaweed lying in a corner by the fence to be spread under the seeds as they were laid. Martin, in spite of the cold, threw off everything above his waist except his striped woollen shirt. Then he spat on his hands, seized his spade and cried: "Now you are going to see what kind of a man you have, Mary."

"There, now," said Mary, tying a little shawl closer under her chin. "Aren't we boastful this early hour of the morning? Maybe I'll wait till sunset to see what kind of a man I have got."

The work began. Martin measured the ground by the southern fence for the first ridge, a strip of ground four feet wide, and he placed the line along the edge and pegged it at each end. Then he spread fresh seaweed over the strip. Mary filled her apron with seeds and began to lay them in rows, four, three, four. When she was a little distance down the ridge, Martin advanced with his spade to the head, eager to commence.

"Now in the name of God," he cried, spitting on his palms, "let us raise the first sod!"

"Oh, Martin, wait till I'm with you!" cried Mary, dropping her seeds on the ridge and running up to him. Her fingers outside her woollen mittens were numb with the cold, and she couldn't wipe them in her apron. Her cheeks seemed to be on fire. She put an arm round Martin's waist and stood looking at the green sod his spade was going to cut, with the excitement of a little child.

"Now for God's sake, girl, keep back!" said Martin gruffly. "Suppose anybody saw us trapesing about like this in the field of our spring sowing, what would they take us for but a pair of useless, soft, empty-headed people that would be sure to die of the hunger. Huh!" He spoke very rapidly, and his eyes were fixed on the ground before him. His eyes had a wild, eager light in them as if some primeval impulse were burning within his brain and driving out every other desire but that of asserting his manhood and of subjugating the earth.

"Oh, what do we care who is looking?" said Mary; but she drew back at the same time and gazed distantly at the ground. Then Martin cut the sod, and pressing the spade deep into the earth with his foot, he turned up the first sod with a crunching sound as the grass roots were dragged out of the earth. Mary sighed and walked back hurriedly to her seeds with furrowed brows. She picked up her seeds and began to spread them rapidly to drive out the sudden terror that had seized her at that moment when the first sod was turned up and she saw the fierce, hard look in her husband's eyes, that were unconscious of her presence. She became suddenly afraid of that pitiless, cruel earth, the peasant's slave master, that would keep her chained to hard work and poverty all her life until she would sink again into its bosom. Her short-lived love was gone. Henceforth she was only her husband's helper to till the earth. And Martin, absolutely without thought, worked furiously, covering the ridge with black earth, his sharp spade gleaming white as he whirled it sideways to beat the sods.

Then, as the sun rose, the little valley beneath the ivy-covered hills became dotted with white frieze shirts, and everywhere men worked madly, without speaking, and women spread seeds. There was no heat in the light of the sun, and there was a sharpness in the still thin air that made the men jump on their spade halts ferociously and beat the sods as if they were living enemies. Birds hopped silently before the spades, with their heads cocked sideways, watching for worms. Made brave by hunger, they often dashed under the spades to secure their food.

Then, when the sun reached a certain point, all the women went back to the village to get dinner for their men, and the men worked on without stopping. Then the women returned, almost running, each carrying a tin can with a flannel tied around it and a little bundle tied with a white cloth. Martin threw down his spade when Mary arrived back in the field. Smiling at one another they sat under the hill for their meal. It was the same as their breakfast, tea and bread and butter.

"Ah," said Martin, when he had taken a long draught of tea from his mug, "is there anything in this world as fine as eating dinner out in the open like this after doing a good morning's work? There, I have done two ridges and a half. That's more than any man in the village could do. Ha!" And he looked at his wife proudly.

"Yes, isn't it lovely," said Mary, looking at the black ridges wistfully. She was just munching her bread and butter. The hurried trip to the village and the trouble of getting the tea ready had robbed her of her appetite. She had to keep blowing at the turf fire with the rim of her skirt, and the smoke nearly blinded her. But now, sitting on that grassy knoll, with the valley all round glistening with fresh seaweed and a light smoke rising from the freshly turned earth, a strange joy swept over her. It overpowered that other feeling of dread that had been with her during the morning.

Martin ate heartily, reveling in his great thirst and his great hunger, with every pore of his body open to the pure air. And he looked around at his neighbors' fields boastfully, comparing them with his own. Then he looked at his wife's little round black head and felt very proud of having her as his own. He leaned back on his elbow and took her hand in his. Shyly and in silence, not knowing what to say and ashamed of their gentle feelings, for peasants are always ashamed of feeling refined, they finished eating and still sat hand in hand looking away into the distance. Everywhere the sowers were resting on little knolls, men, women and children sitting in silence. And the great calm of nature in spring filled the atmosphere around them. Everything seemed to sit still and wait until midday had passed. Only the gleaming sun chased westwards at a mighty pace, in and out through white clouds.

Then in a distant field an old man got up, took his spade and began to clean the earth from it with a piece of stone. The rasping noise carried a long way in the silence. That was the signal for a general rising all along the little valley. Young men stretched themselves and yawned. They walked slowly back to their ridges.

Martin's back and his wrists were getting a little sore, and Mary felt that if she stooped again over her seeds her neck would break, but neither said anything and soon they had forgotten their tiredness in the mechanical movement of their bodies. The strong smell of the upturned earth acted like a drug on their nerves.

In the afternoon, when the sun was strongest, the old men of the village came out to look at their people sowing. Martin's grandfather, almost bent double over his thick stick, stopped in the land outside the field and, groaning loudly, he leaned over the fence.

"God bless the work," he called wheezily.

"And you, grandfather," replied the couple together, but they did not stop working.

"Ha!" muttered the old man to himself. "Ha! He sows well and that woman is good, too. They are beginning well."

It was fifty years since he had begun with his Mary, full of hope and pride, and the merciless soil had hugged them to its bosom ever since, each spring without rest. But he did not think of that. The soil gives forgetfulness. Only the present is remembered in the spring, even by the aged who have spent their lives tilling the earth; so the old man, with his huge red nose and the spotted handkerchief tied around his skull under his black soft felt hat, watched his grandson work and gave him advice.

"Don't cut your sods so long," he would wheeze, "you are putting too much soil on your ridge."

"Ah, woman! Don't plant a seed so near the edge. The stalk will come out sideways."

And they paid no heed to him.

"Ah," grumbled the old man, "in my young days, when men worked from morning till night without tasting food, better work was done. But of course it can't be expected to be the same as it was. The breed is getting weaker. So it is."

Then he began to cough in his chest and hobbled away to another field where his son Michael was working.

By sundown Martin had five ridges finished. He threw down his spade and stretched himself. All his bones ached and he wanted to lie down and rest. "It's time to be going home, Mary," he said.

Mary straightened herself, but she was too tired to reply. She looked at Martin wearily and it seemed to her that it was a great many years since they had set out that morning. Then she thought of the journey home and the trouble of feeding the pigs, putting the fowls into their coops and getting the supper ready, and a momentary flash of rebellion against the slavery of being a peasant's wife crossed her mind. It passed in a moment. Martin was saying, as he dressed himself:

"Ha! My soul from the devil, it has been a good day's work. Five ridges done, and each one of them as straight as a steel rod. Begob, Mary, it's no boasting to say that ye might well be proud of being the wife of Martin Delaney. And that's not saying the whole of it, my girl. You did your share better than any woman in Inverara could do it this blessed day."

They stood for a few moments in silence, looking at the work they had done. All her dissatisfaction and weariness vanished from Mary's mind with the delicious feeling of comfort that overcame her at having done this work with her husband. They had done it together. They had planted seeds in the earth. The next day and the next and all their lives, when spring came they would have to bend their backs and do it until their hands and bones got twisted with rheumatism. But night would always bring sleep and forgetfulness.

As they walked home slowly, Martin walked in front with another peasant talking about the sowing, and Mary walked behind, with her eyes on the ground, thinking.

Cows were lowing at a distance

Acknowledgments

(continued from page ii)

Darhansoff & Verrill Literary Agency: "I Am Not One of Those Who Left the Land" by Anna Akhmatova, from *Poems of Akhmatova*, selected and translated by Stanley Kunitz with Max Hayward. Reprinted by permission of Darhansoff & Verrill Literary Agency.

Devin-Adair Publishers, Inc.: "Spring Sowing" by Liam O'Flaherty, from *The Stories of Liam O'Flaherty*. Copyright © 1956 by Devin-Adair Publishers, Inc. Reprinted by permission of Devin-Adair Publishers, Inc., 6 N. Water Street, Greenwich, CT 06830.